Making Successful Presentations

Making Successful Presentations

A SELF-TEACHING GUIDE

TERRY C. SMITH

A Wiley Press Book
JOHN WILEY & SONS, INC.
New York • Chichester • Brisbane • Toronto • Singapore

To all those
who are about to give
their first presentation

Library of Congress Cataloging in Publication Data:

Smith, Terry C., 1933-
　Making successful presentations.

　(A Self-teaching guide)
　Bibliography: p.
　Includes index
　1. Communication in management. 2. Public speaking.
I. Title. II. Series.
HF5718.S63　1984　　　808.5'1　　　83-23313

ISBN 0-471-88777-3 (pbk.)

Printed in the United States of America

84　85　10　9　8　7

Preface

WHAT IS A PRESENTATION? And how does it differ from an oration, after-dinner speech, or other talks? All are forms of public speaking, so there are similarities. For example, a presenter can be entertaining, but the objective is not entertainment. The presenter cultivates thought, modifies opinions, and promotes action. When you give a presentation, you are selling yourself and your ideas.

In every major city there are thousands of presentations on any given day—from the moment the sun rises until long after it has set. These include presentations in large corporations, talks to civic associations, training seminars, club meetings, customer briefings, workplace meetings, "inspirational" talks to salespeople, and countless others. The audiences at these presentations (particularly those in the business world) are becoming ever more critical of what constitutes a good presentation. At the same time, most of the people giving presentations recognize they need help.

Courses in how to give presentations cost hundreds of dollars—some cost thousands. Few give the breadth of coverage this book is intended to provide. It is designed to show you how to eliminate your fears, gain recognition as a good speaker, and have fun doing it!

This is a how-to book on planning, organizing, developing, and delivering presentations. Included are the basic areas singled out by Aristotle in *The Rhetoric* in 350 B.C.: You (the speaker), the Talk, and most important, the Audience. An additional area, Mechanics (artwork, projectors, etc.), is also covered.

The chapters follow the sequence in which your next presentation will come about, starting with your being asked (or told) to give a talk, and ending with how to handle questions and answers.

Thus, you will have a step-by-step guide that can be applied to presentations you will have to give in the near future. The text is supplemented by artwork showing charts, slides, viewgraphs, room setups, etc. Checklists are also provided at appropriate points.

Perhaps you are wondering if it really takes all of these pages just to cover what to do in a ten- or twenty-minute talk. The answer is *Yes*, and there could have been many more. You won't use every one in every talk you give. But sooner or later, you'll be able to use most of them.

—Terry C. Smith

Acknowledgments

THIS BOOK would not be complete without citing a few of those who have helped point the way.

First, there are those who specialize in teaching the art. Training received from Jim Beveridge, Jack Hilton, Bill Sears, Bill Tacey, Jerry Tarver, and Herb True has proven invaluable. Their earlier work and that of others listed in the Resources and Suggested Reading sections set the stage for my own efforts.

Secondly, there are those experts who, while they do not specialize in teaching the art of presentations in seminars or classrooms, do so day in and day out in the "real world." I'm thankful to have had the opportunity to watch and learn from Mark Braga, Frank Brusca, Tom Burgher, Rick Campbell, Tom Hiller, Suzanne Jenniches, Carol LaRotunda, George Mohr, Paul Pan, Geoff Pevner, Gordon Rowse, Joe Ryan, Al Spencer, Gene Strull, John Stuntz, Jack Tymann, and others, many of whom also reviewed portions of this book.

Finally, and most importantly, one learns by doing. So I would like to thank all the organizations who have been kind enough to ask me to talk and all those who sat in the audience.

Contents

CHAPTER ONE

So You've Been Asked (or Told) to Give a Talk

BEING ASKED TO GIVE a presentation affects different people in different ways. I recently asked a group of fifty professionals to jot down one or two words describing how they felt when they learned they had to give a presentation. Some of their answers were: "Anxiety" . . . "Fear" . . . "Concern over quality" . . . "Uncomfortable" . . . "Oh God!" . . . "Anger" . . . "Apprehension" . . . "Uninteresting" . . . "What did I do to deserve this?" . . . "Why me?" . . . "Inarticulate" . . . "I can't do it" . . . "Flattered" . . . "Extra work" . . . "There goes the weekend" . . . "Hot dog! I'll show them" . . . "How will I find time?" . . . and quite a few "Expletives Deleted."

I find it interesting that the overall reaction was a groan, instead of a "GREAT!" Very few viewed the situation as an opportunity to excel, which it is!

Why are presentations considered so tough? Well, first of all you are singled out as an individual. Although you may have a team to help prepare your presentation, you will be up there alone doing the talking. Second, since you will be seeking acceptance both for yourself and your ideas, you will experience some fear of rejection. So, there is some risk involved both for you as an individual and for the organization you represent.

Tough? You betcha! Impossible? Of course not. Success will lie in control of: yourself, your material, and the environment (including the audience). Various chapters in this book deal with each of these in detail as they occur in the presentation process. For the moment, though, you need to overcome that initial discomfort almost everyone feels when asked (or told) to give a presentation. If you are suffering any anxiety, you share it with some pretty famous people: Erma Bombeck, Lord Laurence Olivier, and even Sally Forth. As for the less famous, there are thousands of presentations being given every day and virtually all of those speakers are part-timers. So you've got lots of company.

Some of the rumblings going on inside your gut at this early stage may be in anticipation of the anxiety you expect to encounter as you approach the lectern. A point to remember is that those rumblings are natural, natural to everyone! In later chapters, you will learn how to minimize those butterflies. But most of these initial rumblings probably are not related to actually making the presentation; rather, they may result from one of the most frequently asked questions on earth.

"WHY ME?"

Were you really surprised that you were asked to give a presentation? With the large number of presentations being given each day, *you should be surprised you weren't asked earlier.*

Chances are the person who asked you to speak considers you to be an expert in your field or in the particular aspect to be addressed. That's right. *You* are the expert. You may have never thought of yourself as such, but everyone has expertise in something. And yours is about to be tapped!

By the same token you must believe in what you are saying. (Are you really interested in the topic? You must be interested in what you have to say in order for others to be. If not, perhaps someone else *should* be giving the talk.) The audience wants to believe in you, and you give them that assurance by showing interest in your topic. Put these two ingredients together—your belief (or interest)

SALLY FORTH   **by Greg Howard**

Sally Forth's fear of speaking

in the topic, and the audience's belief in you—and a chemical reaction will occur. You will come across as a real person with something important to say.

Why give an oral presentation at all? Why not hand out a photocopy, or if the budget permits, a nice, color brochure? The answer is because these things simply can't match the impact of a live presentation given by a lively individual. The "you" element is crucial. In today's hectic world many people can't be reached by the written word. Their schedules simply won't allow them to peruse written reports chock-full of charts, schematics, and diagrams. Figuratively, you sometimes have to grab them by their lapels in order to get their attention. Couple this with our society's addiction to television and you can see that we really do live in an audio-visual age.

The presentation is a creature of this age.

A presentation is not a lecture. Of course, part of your objective may be to inform, but you usually need to gain information from the audience as well and possibly persuade them to take some action. A presentation is an exercise in interaction, with the speaker presenting new ideas in an attractive, interesting way.

Considering the opportunity the speaker has to adjust to a particular audience, and the ability to engage in dialogue, you can see we are dealing with a very powerful communications tool. Indeed, the word *communication* has a heritage of imparting, participating, and commonality. One of its nearby neighbors in the dictionary is *communion*, which signifies mutual participation or sharing of ideas or feelings. All of these elements are present in a good presentation.

WHAT A GOOD PRESENTATION CAN DO

History is full of disasters that could have been prevented by better communication (Little Big Horn, Pearl Harbor, Kent State). There may be similar disasters—large and small—lurking in the wings at your organization. Whether you are in the business of raising funds, managing an organization, or dealing with government agencies, success depends upon your ability to communicate effectively. How many opportunities have you seen lost because of a poor oral presentation? How many times have you walked away from the lectern unsure of how well you reached your audience? Was the subject a *now* topic, of immediate use? Did it stimulate any dialogue? Was the audience motivated to take action?

A good presentation can be very rewarding:

- The benefits for the audience can involve ways to save time or money, or how to make their lives easier or more successful.
- Your organization can benefit in funding being made available or a contract that is won.
- You benefit from the recognition that comes from making all this happen.

Companies realize that good speakers are a valuable asset. With a few good presentations and some luck, you may find yourself hurried along the road to prominence and promotion.

And yet there are so many examples of people who have failed to live up to their potential simply because they let their fear of public speaking hold them back. Ask yourself, are you so terrified of speaking in public that you would prefer to let others succeed in your place rather than take a chance on yourself? If the answer is yes, go back to your bookstore and buy a book on assertiveness!

WHAT WILL IT TAKE TO IMPROVE?

Unfortunately, there is no magic formula or potion. If there were, this book could have been condensed into an article or perhaps an illustration. Instead of five steps to a good presentation, there are hundreds, and you'll find as many of them as I could think of in this book. Fortunately, none of them are extremely difficult; they do, however, require a commitment to improving your presentation skills.

In giving a presentation your goal is perfection. You want to give a talk where the audience not only shows up, but participates and leaves feeling satisfied, taking some new ideas with them, and inspired to do something. You also want to give one in which all the taken-for-granted mechanics go off without a hitch. This is perfection! *And you and I will probably never see it!*

On the other hand, the very bottom of the scale, the worst talk I ever saw consisted of a script that took one and one-half hours to read and was accompanied by only five visuals which were either unreadable or irrelevant. Certainly, your next talk is going to be better than that one. Indeed, you'll probably be pretty good. And, by the time you've had a chance to combine some of the principles in this book with your own desire to improve, you are going to be terrific.

You've Already Gotten a Big Start

Speaking is a skill you've been practicing all your life. But your experience in daily life has been mostly of one-on-one interactions. Standing before a group is different.

But is speaking to a group really that much different? Place yourself in the audience. Wouldn't you prefer being talked to as an individual? And what's to prevent a speaker from singling out members of the audience, either through eye contact or direct address, and speaking to one person for a while before switching to someone else. This one-on-one approach can have a beneficial effect on both the audience and the speaker, particularly if the speaker begins by selecting individuals he or she already knows and is comfortable with.

Certainly, speaking before a group is a learned skill. If you aspire to become a "golden throat," it will take years of training. But I strongly believe almost anyone can make a good presentation if he or she knows the subject, sets high standards for the talk, and is willing to work hard in preparation. All of us are equipped with the required tools—mind and voice. How we use them can separate us from the crowd.

One Hour for Every Minute

According to *Best Sermons*, a religious magazine, it takes clergymen about seven hours to prepare a twenty-minute talk. That's more than a twenty-to-one ratio. But if twenty people are going to be listening to that sermon, it merely represents an equal tradeoff of time spent preparing versus their total time listening.

Business presentations require the same or an even higher ratio. Here, the *value* of the presentation establishes the ratio. I subscribe to the theory of making things harder for myself in order to make them easier for my audience. For a brand new presentation, my ratio is one hour of preparation for every minute I plan to speak. This is the preparation level at which I feel comfortable that I'm giving my very best.

Mark Twain once said, "It takes three weeks to prepare a good ad-lib speech." And I'm sure you're familiar with Abraham Lincoln's immortal Gettysburg Address. Only 266 words were delivered from a few notes scribbled on an envelope during his train ride. Originally, some people were offended by the brevity of Lincoln's speech. Later, historians found many drafts in Lincoln's own handwriting which showed that weeks of effort went into that speech, which took but four minutes to deliver, but will be remembered for hundreds of years.

In his "Meeting Clinic" column in *Successful Meetings* magazine, Coleman Finkel, president of National Conference Centers, was asked how long he thought a speaker should take to prepare a thirty-minute talk. His response was:

> I will answer your question by identifying the steps that should be followed in preparing a talk. I cannot give you a definitive answer because it will depend on individual factors.
>
> a. Experience and skill of individual in preparing and giving talks.
> b. Knowledge of subject matter.
> c. Help that individual will have in preparing talk.
> d. References available for consultation and research on subject of talk: colleagues, library, authorities.
> e. Whether speaker requires full text or outline.
>
> The steps used in preparing a talk are as follows:
>
> a. Identify the areas in which you want to do fact-gathering and define the scope of your subject.
>   I find this step important so that you have some direction in which to proceed. The scope tells you the framework within which your talk will be developed. Check at this point with the program coordinator to see if the direction that you are taking is one that she/he had in mind.
> b. Gather information on the subject.
>   Make notes from library research, reading in magazines and books. Talk to colleagues; call authorities to get their ideas on the subject.
> c. Pull out of your research the key ideas that you believe are important.
> d. Write an outline in the sequence in which you feel the subject should logically be developed.
> e. Show it to colleagues for comments.
> f. Rehearse giving your talk aloud.
> g. Give to spouse, friends, or colleagues and ask for critical comment.
> h. Decide on where and what kind of visuals will be used.
> i. Refine talk and practice until you have absorbed the key points and you feel at ease with the talk.
>
> In the preparation I make for talks, I follow the above sequence but it may be spread over a couple of months. I like to get to work immediately on a presentation and let it mull around in my mind. I don't like the pressure of last-minute preparation. I don't think you can do your best by waiting until the zero hour. *In concentrated time, it takes me about one to two weeks to prepare a thirty minute talk.*[1] [Emphasis added.]

So you can easily see where all that time goes. As Finkel says, it's nice to be able to spread the effort out over a couple of months, but what if you *have* to give your talk tomorrow? If there's absolutely no way out, here's how you might be able to do it and survive. First, isolate yourself so you'll be free from any possible interruptions. Second, adopt a technique the poker players in Las Vegas use. They don't think in terms of thousands of dollars because it might be too

TIME ALLOCATION FOR PRESENTATION PREPARATION

Units	%	Activity	Comments
1	2	Review the objective	Check with whoever asked (or told) you to speak. Make sure you are both on the same track. Put it in writing.
2	3	Analyze the audience	What do they need (or want) to know? What are their educations, backgrounds, interests? Who are the "friendlies"? "Hostiles"?
2	3	Look for help	Has anyone talked to this group before? Are any existing visuals available? Can you get help with the legwork?
10	17	Research the subject	Collect facts and figures. Look for quotes from authorities. Search out appropriate anecdotes.
1	2	Settle on a theme	What is the main point? How does it match your objective? Can you condense your message to a single point?
3	5	Outline/organize	Begin to put material in logical order. Look for gaps and inconsistencies. Where is it weak? Use as a checklist.
8	13	Prepare storyboards/ script	Put narration and visuals together on a single sheet. Do they work together to present the same idea?
7	12	Practice	Go over the material once all by yourself, reading it out loud. Tape-record if possible. How does it sound? Go over it again.
5	8	Revise storyboards	Review storyboards and look for improvements based on results of practice session.
5	8	Dry run	Give presentation to a group of friends or colleagues, using storyboard art for visuals. Ask for pluses and minuses. Check time required.
5	8	Revise storyboards	Incorporate suggestions made during dry run. Strengthen any weak or confusing areas.
8	14	Prepare visuals	Prepare the most effective visuals you can within the constraints of time and money. Check them carefully.
3	5	Rehearse	Using the same group as before, give your narration and visuals one last runthrough. Check time required. Fine-tune if necessary.
60	100%		

frightening. Instead they think in terms of units. Likewise, don't think of your available time in terms of hours. Whatever the available time is, divide it into sixty units as shown in the table on page 7. (Sixty was chosen since it will correlate nicely with any number of minutes or hours you have available. The more conventional percentage values are also listed.) Feel free to make adjustments. For example, you might want to increase the amount of time spent on research. Fine, but keep in mind you need to be able to bring personal expertise to the talk. If you have to spend too much time on research, you may not be the right person to be the "expert." If you can obtain help on research or the preparation of final visuals, you can add the units saved to other categories. If absolutely necessary, you can prepare quickie viewgraphs directly from your storyboards, again freeing units of time for other activities on the chart. But I would caution against strengthening one area at the expense of eliminating or neglecting another. For example, I would strongly advise against attempting to combine the practice, the dry run, and the rehearsal into a single activity. Doing all three separately is designed to build a degree of confidence you will enjoy having when you speak to your real audience.

You will find each of the activities in this table discussed in detail in the remaining chapters of this book. But before we close out this introductory chapter, I would like to relate a demonstration that Jack Felton, vice-president for corporate communications of a large multinational firm, uses in his talks on communications. Jack passes out little bags of confetti and asks the audience to take a pinch between their fingers and let it drop to the floor. He then points out that their particular message is just one little flake in the ensuing snowstorm that we refer to as the information explosion— so the message had better be good if they want it to be noticed, received, and understood! Then, after the confetti has reached the floor, he asks everyone to compare the pattern of their confetti with those on both sides. Each, of course, is different—just as each of us are, and so are our messages.

Throughout this book we will be giving you lots of suggestions. But in the end it will be *your* talk. You will have to select what works best for you. And when those things start working for you, there will be one more step in our confetti analogy—*celebration!*

Just like anything else, the more involved you become in presentations, the better you will become. And you can start right now!

CHAPTER TWO

Planning: "Who, What, Where, When, Why, and How?"

PLANNING—THE PROFESSIONAL APPROACH

ALMOST EVERYTHING we come in contact with testifies to the importance of planning. At work, at home, or at play, planning is everywhere—planning, or the lack of it, is easy to spot.

Why is poor planning so easy to spot? The answer is quality; it's the difference between a home gardener and a landscaper. Planning is the professional approach. Every professional—every architect, engineer, purchasing agent, and accountant—knows the importance of planning, and would never think of working without a plan. It's almost impossible to achieve quality without planning.

Why, then, do we often neglect this facet in presentations? Every talk is a unique experience and requires individual planning. Mistakes, misdirection, or lack of attention at this stage will take you farther and farther off course as you proceed.

Planning can be an involved process, and that (plus its importance) is why this entire chapter is devoted to it. However, to simplify things, six aspects of planning are covered. These are the six questions learned by every cub reporter: who, what, where, when, why, and how. (Many feature journalists add an all-important seventh point: WOW!) Your ability to answer these questions now is every bit as important as your ability to answer those asked by your audience at the end of your talk.

THE NO. 1 CAUSE OF POOR PRESENTATIONS

Although your talk obviously isn't very far along at this point, you have a chance right now to eliminate the number one cause of poor presentations. At this stage most speakers concentrate on the *what* in their presentations. They ask themselves, "What in the world am I going to say?" and jumping to that question is often the biggest mistake that can be made. Instead of *what*, the question should be *why*.

WHY AM I GIVING THIS TALK?

"Because I have to," is *not* a good reason for giving a presentation. What you need to begin creating a good presentation is an objective. There can be many objectives in giving a talk. Perhaps you want to:

- Inform or instruct.
- Persuade or sell.
- Make recommendations and gain acceptance.
- Arouse interest.
- Inspire or initiate action.
- Evaluate, interpret, or clarify.
- Set the stage for further action.
- Gather ideas and explore them.
- Entertain.

Perhaps you are aiming for a combination of these. For example, there is nothing wrong with being both informative *and* entertaining—the two are not mutually exclusive. In fact, the two may complement one another.

Note that these are fairly *general* objectives. This is a good start, but you'll need to be more specific. One way to do this is to put your objective in writing. Many times I've sat in lengthy planning meetings where apparently everybody had finally reached agreement, and someone said, "Well, I guess that about wraps it up," half rising from his chair—only to be stopped by an, "I wonder if we could capture that objective in writing on the chalkboard." The result is usually a unanimous moan at the prospect of spending any more time on planning rather than doing. Unfortunately, the result frequently is also the inability to capture in specific terms the objective that had seemed so clear just minutes ago.

Putting objectives in writing can keep you from deluding yourself. Written objectives can also provide a "contract" between you and your superiors. And they can provide the theme for your entire presentation.

The specific purpose of a speech must be established before any other preparation is started. It should be written in infinitive phrase form something like this example: "To inform the members of Local 306 how observing the rules of parliamentary debate can help assure that all points of view can be expressed by members in union meetings." Once it is written, examine it carefully to determine if it expresses accurately why you want to speak. Revision may be necessary to be certain that the scope of the topic is narrow enough to be covered in the time allotted.[2]

This quote, from William Tacey's *Business and Professional Speaking*, provides a lot of good advice, and I would like to add some more of my own. Starting your written objective with an infinitive phrase is the best way to begin; but while "to inform" is all right, also consider such phrases as "to convince," "to persuade," "to show," "to prove," or "to demonstrate." They make writing your objective a little tougher, but they are usually more realistic. Also, don't be dismayed if your objective is not as succinct as the one cited above. Your first cut may be three times as long as you want it to be, and careful distillation is necessary. If you hit it right off the bat, you had better be suspicious. Writing a *good* objective is harder than you think. Here are some more samples:

- To prove that purchase of a Humdinger-999 will permit the combination of several other data handling systems and supply more complete data usable by all departments at a savings of $35,000 per year in reduced personnel and rentals.
- To demonstrate to the director and staff the need for a new educational program for the disadvantaged in District Three, and to obtain an $80,000 budgetary allocation for Phase I.
- To convince the capital equipment committee that installing robotic paint spraying equipment in Building Twenty-three will increase productivity thirty-eight percent, pay for itself in three years, and eliminate a hazardous working condition.
- To persuade the swim club committee that purchasing a new filter at the end of the season will result in a lower price and guarantee its delivery prior to next year, thus avoiding a possible shutdown.

If you have help in formulating your objective, so much the better. But you may find yourself stuck with a vague assignment. "Bob, work up a talk on the new electronic mail system for our sales reps," or "Could you talk about 'Publishing Today' to our Careers Group?" Converting these command performances on fuzzy, general topics into your own, tailored-to-the-audience's-needs presentation will require a well-thought-out objective.

One way to make writing that objective easier is to visualize the end of your talk. What do you want to happen? Applause would be nice, but it's unlikely in most presentations. Beyond that what do you want your audience to take with them or do?

- Should they be taking something with them that will help them do their jobs better?
- What is going to be different from the way it was before you gave your talk?
- Will they give you their "votes"?
- What decisions will they need to make and when?
- Will morale improve?
- Will productivity increase?

As you develop your written objective, there are two criteria you should apply:

1. Is it attainable?
2. Is it measurable?

Writing an objective that is not attainable, realistic, or feasible will either guarantee failure or provide you with a convenient cop-out: "Oh well, we really didn't expect to achieve a behavioral change with just one meeting anyway."

Here, the problem is often due to multiple objectives. Multiple objectives require multiple talks. Limiting yourself to a single objective (or two at the most) will make your task much easier. Often, attaining goals is like eating a dinosaur. It's best done one bite at a time.

The second item, measurability, is going to make your life more difficult. In order for the results of your presentation to be verifiable, they must be measurable. Sometimes the results are obvious and immediate. You get a "Yes" or a "Go-ahead." Other times you will need a quantitative method of evaluating results. In a training session, a quiz can measure information transfer. Increased orders from the sales force would be a nice, easily measurable result. So would the percentage of attendees filling out a new form correctly. A before-and-after survey would indicate change. And, there's always getting reelected. Whatever the situation, try to find a way of measuring results, and incorporate the intended amount of change in your objective.

WHO IS GOING TO BE OUT THERE?

Remembering that Aristotle singled out the audience as the most important of the three elements in a talk (*You*, the *Talk* itself, and the *Audience*), you should consider the *who* element next.

Your audience might be quite small, say a handful of department heads. Or, it may consist of all the employees in a department. Regardless of its size, it is virtually impossible for you to know too much about your audience. You need to analyze their ages, educations, backgrounds, interests, and—particularly—their needs, so that you can look at your talk from *their* viewpoint.

In his prologue to *The Inconstant*, George Farquhar wrote, "Like hungry guests, a sitting audience looks." Don't send them away hungry. Satisfy their needs.

In the business world, management is primarily interested in four principal factors:

- Reducing costs
- Improving quality
- Shortening schedules
- Increasing performance

All four of these primary interests would obviously need to be considered in planning a presentation to management. Behind them lie a myriad of other interests, needs, problems, and beliefs that would apply to management or any broader audience. These read like alphabet soup. Refer to the table on page 14. Scan the list slowly, and as you do, check off those items that seem to fit both your audience and your objective.

Two things are beginning to happen. First, you are beginning to mesh your objective with the audience. Ideally, they fit together like well-turned gears. Second, you are beginning to look at your audience as individuals. Certainly, your objective will have an impact on how you "handle" the audience. In some portions of your talk, you may be forced to generalize for the benefit of the entire audience. During other portions you'll want to home in on specific individuals. Looking at your audience as a homogenous group is invariably a mistake. If you find yourself doing this, more homework is in order.

You want to "give" everyone in your audience something, and (if possible) not step on anybody's toes. Doing this requires an individual approach.

If you already know everyone in your audience, you have a pretty good start. Perhaps the audience is a committee that will have to approve your design or request. Chances are that their

AUDIENCE INTERESTS AND CONCERNS

_____ ABSENTEEISM
_____ ACCEPTANCE
_____ ACCOMPLISHMENTS
_____ ADVANCEMENT
_____ AGE
_____ AMBITION
_____ ANNOUNCEMENTS
_____ APPEARANCE
_____ APPROVAL
_____ ATTITUDE
_____ AUTHORITY
_____ AWARDS

_____ BEAUTY
_____ BELIEFS
_____ BENEFITS
_____ BIASES
_____ BUSINESS

_____ CAUSES
_____ CAUTION
_____ CHANGE
_____ CHARACTER
_____ CLIENTS
_____ CLIMATE
_____ COHESIVENESS
_____ COMMUNITY
_____ COMPETITION
_____ CONSCIENCE
_____ CONSOLIDATION
_____ COST
_____ COURTESY
_____ CRITICISM
_____ CUSTOMERS

_____ DATA
_____ DELAYS
_____ DEPENDABILITY
_____ DESIGN
_____ DEVOTION
_____ DISTINCTION
_____ DURABILITY
_____ DUTY

_____ ECONOMY
_____ EDUCATION
_____ EFFORT
_____ EMPLOYEES
_____ EMPLOYMENT
_____ ENERGY
_____ ENTERTAINMENT
_____ ENVY
_____ EQUIPMENT
_____ ETHICS
_____ EXCLUSIVENESS
_____ EXPECTATIONS
_____ EXPENSE
_____ EXPERIENCES

_____ FACILITIES
_____ FAIRNESS
_____ FAMILY

_____ FEAR
_____ FORCE
_____ FORMALITY
_____ FRIENDLINESS

_____ GAIN
_____ GOOD WILL
_____ GREED
_____ GROUP EFFORT

_____ HANDLING
_____ HEALTH
_____ HISTORY
_____ HOMELIFE
_____ HOPE
_____ HOUSING
_____ HUMOR

_____ IMAGE
_____ INCOME
_____ INDIVIDUALITY
_____ INFLUENCE
_____ INSPIRATION

_____ JEALOUSY

_____ KNOWLEDGE

_____ LABOR
_____ LEGALITY
_____ LOCATION
_____ LOST TIME
_____ LOVE
_____ LOW COST
_____ LOYALTY

_____ MAINTENANCE
_____ MANAGEMENT
_____ MARITAL STATUS
_____ MATERIAL
_____ MISCONCEPTIONS
_____ MOOD
_____ MORALE
_____ MORALITY
_____ MOTIVATION

_____ NATIONALISM
_____ NEEDS
_____ NEWNESS

_____ OBJECTIVES
_____ OPINIONS
_____ OPPORTUNITIES
_____ ORGANIZATION

_____ PAROCHIALISM
_____ PARTICIPATION
_____ PAY
_____ PEOPLE
_____ PERFORMANCE
_____ PERSONALITY
_____ PLANNING

_____ POLICIES
_____ POPULARITY
_____ POSITION
_____ POWER
_____ PRAISE
_____ PREJUDICE
_____ PRIDE
_____ PROBLEMS
_____ PRODUCIBILITY
_____ PRODUCTIVITY
_____ PROFIT
_____ PROMOTION
_____ PROSPERITY
_____ PROTECTION
_____ PUBLIC
_____ PURITY

_____ QUALITY

_____ RANK
_____ RECREATION
_____ RELAXATION
_____ RELIABILITY
_____ REPAIR
_____ REPUTATION
_____ RESEARCH
_____ RULES

_____ SAFETY
_____ SALARY
_____ SALES
_____ SCHEDULE
_____ SECURITY
_____ SELF-RESPECT
_____ SERVICE
_____ SIZE
_____ SOCIABILITY
_____ SOPHISTICATION
_____ STANDARDS
_____ STRATEGIES
_____ STYLE
_____ SUCCESS
_____ SUPERIORITY
_____ SUPPORT
_____ SYMPATHY

_____ TECHNOLOGY
_____ TIMELINESS
_____ TOOLS

_____ UNDERSTANDING
_____ UNITY
_____ USEFULNESS

_____ VALUE
_____ VANITY

_____ WAGES
_____ WELFARE
_____ WORKLOAD
_____ WORSHIP

_____ YOUTH

responsibilities (financial, operational, etc.) will tell you what their individual interests are, allowing you to build portions of your talk around those interests. Also, you may have seen them in other meetings, giving you a chance to analyze their personalities. Which individual requires the thought-out approach? Who is more likely to be captured by a creative idea? Do any of them look on pizzazz as gimmickry? Make these items factors when you consider your approach to the presentation.

What if they are total strangers? Well, your job just got a lot tougher, but not impossible. There are still lots of things you can do:

- Ask for a list of likely attendees and their titles. And, while you're at it, ask for first names—not initials. Paste a copy next to your bathroom mirror and another next to your office phone. Look at them every chance you get. Study them in groups of three. Study them forwards and backwards, matching first name to last name to position, and vice versa. When you finally meet them, they will seem like old friends.
- If possible, get their biographies or personal histories. If your audience is going to be customers at a far-off location, perhaps your field sales representative can help.
- Talk to as many of them as possible in advance. Ask them about their biggest challenges or problems. Talk about what they would like to see at this particular meeting. Ask them what they liked or disliked at previous meetings. Look for ways to incorporate their views in your talk, and ways to meet their objections.

You owe your audience a worthwhile message that is well-presented. In order to deliver, you're going to have to know as much about them as possible. Will they be friendly, but likely to ask probing questions? Will they be hostile? You've got to be prepared!

WHAT AM I GOING TO SAY?

You've probably known the general topic of your talk ever since you were asked (or told) to speak. And, having written out your objective and analyzed your audience, you now have a fair idea of what might be included under your topic.

We will be talking about gathering and organizing information in more detail in the next chapter. For now, you can ask yourself a few more *whats*:

- What do they already know?
- What do they want to know?
- What do they need to know?
- What don't they need to know?
- What shouldn't (or can't) I talk about?

The fourth question refers to too much detail, or (as is the case with many novice speakers), trying to cover the whole world in a single talk. Leave the epics for James Michener and Herman Wouk. Pick one aspect of a subject you are familiar with, that the audience is interested in, and that fits your objective. That's the magic formula.

The "shouldn't" in the final question refers to sensitive information that you would not bring up, but would be prepared to handle if it surfaced during the question-and-answer session. The "can't" refers to information outside your area of responsibility that might be inappropriate for you to comment on.

WHERE WILL THE MEETING BE?

You need to know more than just where to show up. We will be talking about room arrangements in Chapter 8, but there are some items you should start thinking about now. First of all, make sure the meeting room is reserved. With the large number of meetings being held these days, suitable rooms are scarce. They need to be reserved as far in advance as possible. If it's not your responsibility and someone else has reserved the room, double-check. If at all possible, visit the room. Will it handle your group comfortably? (If it's in a hotel, don't trust their seating numbers unless you're hosting a brotherhood meeting for leprechauns.) What type of seating and visuals will work best? What kind of audio-visual equipment is available? All of these items are covered elsewhere in this book, but it's not too early to start thinking about them.

There is a special type of talk that takes its name from where it is held. It's called a "workplace meeting." Usually these brief meetings are held right in the workplace. *But they don't have to be.* You can frequently add some importance—even prestige—by getting the meeting away from the workplace. This could be as simple as going outside on the grass or a patio, or using an executive meeting room employees don't usually have access to. You might even want to consider an off-site location.

Perhaps you will be traveling out of town to give your talk. If so, make your travel reservations as far in advance as possible, and don't plan to catch the last possible flight. Reserve a seat on the preceding one and leave yourself a safety cushion in case of weather or equipment problems.

One final *where* on out-of-town meetings—know where you can find help locally. Before you leave home, make sure you have the phone numbers of local sales representatives, the meeting coordinator, the hotel, the audio-visual supplier, and others. Keep in mind that you will need phone numbers to reach these people during business hours, plus an *emergency* number.

WHEN WILL THE MEETING BE?

Here again, you're interested in more than just knowing when to show up. You need to know how much time you have available to speak, and how much time will be available to prepare. In both cases you will have to balance the time you have with the time you need. Furthermore, you will also have to factor in *how long you can keep the audience interested*.

Suppose you've been given a single hour to talk about a project you've been working on for the past five years! You say there's no way you can possibly do it? Tough! In fact, an hour might be *too much*. If you have even the slightest doubt that you can keep the audience interested for that full hour, you would be smart to request that your time be cut back. Remember, the effectiveness of a presentation often varies inversely with the time required to give it. George Plimpton has written very effectively about this:

> As anyone who listens to speeches knows, brevity is an asset. Twenty minutes are ideal. An hour is the limit an audience can listen comfortably.
>
> In mentioning brevity, it is worth mentioning that the shortest inaugural address was George Washington's—just 135 words. The longest was William Henry Harrison's, in 1841. He delivered a two-hour, 9,000-word speech into the teeth of a freezing northeast wind. He came down with a cold the following day, and a month later he died of pneumonia.[3]

Remember, there is no such thing as a captive audience. Even in an employer/employee or teacher/student relationship where you may be able to hold their bodies "captive," you cannot assume you also have their minds. As Mark Twain said, "No sinner is ever saved after the first twenty minutes of a sermon."

Time management is important for speakers, too. Don't try to do too much in the time available. As mentioned previously, don't try to cover "the whole world." Stick to what's going on in your own "home town." That's probably where your audience is coming from anyway.

When will also tell you the time of day you will be speaking. First thing in the morning? Good, with the possible exception of Mondays. Right before lunch? Bad, because they are likely to be tired, hungry, and checking their watches. Right after lunch? Better, they've had a long break and, hopefully, not too heavy a meal. End of the day? Terrible! They're tired and you may be, too. In this slot, only excellence will do—particularly on Fridays. Planning an after-dinner talk? Okay if they've been home and have come back to, say, the local school or library. But if it's a business meeting where alcoholic beverages will be served, try for *between* cocktails and dinner. Sometimes the combination of cocktails, hors d'oeuvres, dinner, and wine leaves you with an audience that Bill Cosby would have trouble keeping awake.

You may not get to pick your time. But you *can* make requests and suggestions. For example, if an organization that meets weekly or monthly asks you to speak, but hasn't given you enough time to prepare adequately (or to get the necessary reviews and approvals if you represent an organization), tell them you'll be happy to do it, but would like to wait until the following session. They get the "yes" they wanted, and you get the time you need.

HOW AM I GOING TO DO IT?

Fortunately, the answer is that you won't have to do it all by yourself. Commercial artists and professional speechwriters are well worth their fees if you or your organization can afford them. And if you can't, you may be able to find some who will waive their fees because they believe in your cause.

There are many other people available who might help. Enlist the aid of friends, family members, your co-workers, your boss, and (possibly) the organization you will be speaking to. Check with your local community college to see if a speech or English teacher would be willing to help. Or ask your pastor. Or, if your talk has any connection with what your company does, ask the people in its public relations or advertising department. Finally, you could contact your local Toastmasters' organization. There's plenty of inexpensive or even free help out there. All you have to do is ask.

Okay, you've given some thought to the famous five W's, particularly where you want to go and why. The rest of this book will show you how to get there.

CHAPTER THREE

Getting Your Act Together: Gathering and Organizing

SOME BOOKS on presentations combine the previous chapter on planning with this one on gathering and organizing. I have elected to treat them separately in order to make the smaller, individual pieces more digestible. But, more importantly, I have divided them because of their individual significance. In the last chapter you laid the concrete foundation for your talk. Now you will begin putting together all those bricks that make up the walls. First, however, you have to find those bricks.

I once heard of a college course in creativity wherein the professor gave each attendee a brick as part of the final exam and told the students to spend the next hour listing every possible use for it they could think of, other than as a building material. Of course, some immediately come to mind: paperweight, weapon, etc. Then there's window prop, measuring device, heat retainer, and so forth. By the end of the hour, the brighter students had each come up with more than 100 uses, proving that even with such a simple subject as a brick, there's no shortage of ideas; all you have to do is capture them.

CAPTURING IDEAS

In *Executive Speaking—An Acquired Skill*, author Joe Powell presents a simple, low-cost method for capturing ideas. "Arm yourself with blank three-by-five cards. I call them idea cards. Whenever and wherever you get an idea jot it down in the rough, one idea to one card. Forget about spelling or grammar. Just jot down every related raw idea; and capture it immediately because ideas, like snowflakes on a mild day in early spring, disappear on contact."[4] So keep those cards with you at all times. There's no telling where or when an idea will arise.

Some of these ideas will no doubt lead to further research. After all, the audience isn't interested merely in your opinions—they also want facts. Facts that you can gather through:

- Literature searches.
- Personal observations.
- Experimentation.
- Questionnaires.
- Interviews.

All of these are part of doing your homework. In his book *How to Write, Speak, and Think More Effectively*, Rudolf Flesch, one of the pioneers in the field, said, "The only thing that's good enough is to soak yourself in all the facts you can lay your hands on, to become a temporary expert on the subject. You go after the most obvious sources, then after the less obvious sources, and finally you follow up all the stray leads that you can possibly uncover. . . . Legwork is nine-tenths of the job."[5]

Your literature search may yield some quotes from famous people or recognized authorities, anecdotes, analogies, jokes and one-liners, cartoons and other visuals, dramatic statistics, clever twists on words, interesting "for examples," and don't forget the bait, which is what I call the benefits your audience will obtain if they follow your advice. Your public library is a treasure house of books, magazines, and newspapers that will help. Some of them are listed in the bibliography of this book; how to use them is covered in the next chapter.

And don't forget to take note paper with you every time you go to hear someone give a lecture, talk, or presentation so that you can capture any outstanding techniques and ideas.

Collect a lot more material than you will ever need. That way your talk will represent the cream of the crop.

Interviews and questionnaires are another way to get information, and they provide a means of testing the water—particularly if they involve people who will be in your audience. Decisionmakers are usually glad to help and somewhat flattered to be asked their opinions. Do your homework. Have plenty of questions ready for when the conversation wanes.

As part of the process of interviewing, you may uncover some objections to the position you are presenting (which you will have to work around or overcome). And, when those who objected finally hear the talk, they will recognize the incorporation of their ideas and, hopefully, become members of your team. Speaking of objections, don't neglect alternative approaches or solutions. And don't neglect the "cons" that go along with your "pros." Show that you have considered them and why you set them aside.

Obviously some of the material you gather is going to be too voluminous to put on those little 3 by 5 cards that Joe Powell recommended. But be sure to make a list of the main points on a card and file the rest of your source materials. Accordion-style file folders work great for storing your resources, or you might try a three-ring binder or even large envelopes. Think of this as your information warehouse.

As you gather your data, subject it to a value analysis:

- How recent?
- How objective?
- How authoritative?
- How accurate?

Bits of data are like children: once you adopt them, they're yours. So be selective. Sift through your material, picking the most relevant and thought-provoking. But don't clean out the warehouse yet. Just because a piece of material isn't going to make it into the main body of your talk doesn't mean that it's worthless. Some of that material may provide valuable ammunition in preparing for the question-and-answer session that will follow your talk.

ORGANIZING YOUR MATERIAL

Many authorities on public speaking suggest that you organize by beginning at the ending. This will help to keep your main objective in mind, minimize detours en route, and avoid the possibility of an anti-climactic ending.

Another approach is to use the thesis mentioned in Chapter 2 as a "screen" and attempt to "fit" your material through this screen as shown in the illustration on page 22. The bits and pieces represent different facts. Those that can go through the screen will fit your talk. Those that don't, won't. The various holes in the screen represent categories; when the material passes through them, it begins to take on an organizational form.

There are two other approaches you can take in organizing your material:

- Organizing to suit the material and its treatment
- Organizing to suit the audience

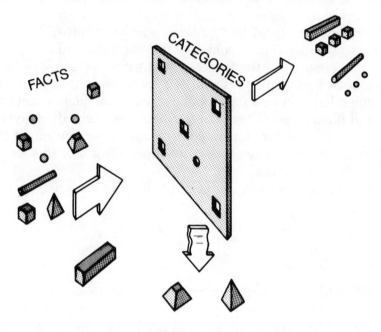

Thesis screen provides filter and preliminary organization.

The best approach is a combination of these two. The following is a discussion of both.

Organizing to Suit the Material

As you sift through the material, certain expository techniques will begin to suggest themselves. The material will begin to divide itself along certain lines. Some of these include:

- Geographical (sales territories, plant locations)
- Organizational (hierarchy, duties)
- Categorical (types, sizes, etc.)
- Appearance (recognition of aircraft, boats, flowers)
- Historical (chronological order of occurrence)
- Operational Cycle (engines, pumps)
- Assembly Sequence (manufacturing or installation instructions)

I'm sure you can see that some of these categories are closely related. For example, business *organizations* are often based on *geographical* plant locations; *appearance* is often *categorized*; and, *historical, operational,* and *assembly* all bear a *chronological* relationship. In fact, chronological organization is the type most frequently used, but not always because it serves us best.

Organizing to Suit the Audience

There are cases where *chronological* organization offers a perfect match between audience and objective. Usually these situations involve repeatability—that is, when you want to make sure a step-by-step procedure is followed in assembling or testing some equipment. In other cases, chronological organization is used merely for convenience. It's quite easy to determine what happened first, and then next, and so forth.

In both *chronological* and *historical* organization, the facts are presented in the order in which they happened, with no concern for relative importance. And there's the rub. Your listeners are kept waiting to learn the important facts.

Climactic organization is used by some speakers who are real spellbinders. It derives from novels and other types of entertaining storytelling. With this organization, the plot builds to a high point (or climax) and then drops off quickly. The highlights are kept from the audience until the end, and since they are being entertained (and have some time to spare), they don't mind waiting.

With *deductive* organization, each fact builds on the previous one until an inescapable conclusion is reached. Loved by lawyers (they know the jury can't leave), this organization is fine for presenting a case or offering proof, and it may come in handy for a really tough sell because it starts on familiar ground that the audience already knows or agrees with. But, like the others, it keeps your listeners waiting. Before using this format, you should be certain they will stick around (both in mind and body) for your entire presentation.

The *learning pattern* organization also uses the technique of relating new material to already familiar material. For example, an electrician attempting to learn how an electronic circuit works will first relate it to prior knowledge of common electrical circuits. As a speaker, you can often take advantage of the audience's prior experience to help get new points across.

One final means of organization is the *qualitative* format (also called the *pyramid*). It is called qualitative because the emphasis is on quality rather than quantity. Emphasis is placed on the important items and these items are discussed up front at the very beginning. Like a newspaper article, the pyramid style gives you the point at the very top (the headline), keeps your interest (with the lead), and then gives you the details (in the body). This style is designed for people who may be too busy to *read* all about it in a report or proposal, and would like someone to merely tell or show them what's important.

Each of these five formats has its own special purpose. The qualitative approach, however, is almost always best for straightforward communication of facts.

Specific Organizational Techniques

Here are some time-tested organizational techniques that embody these principles. At least a few of them should fit your situation:

- The Descriptive Approach (What is it? What does it do? How does it do it?)
- The Events Approach (What happened? Why did it happen? So what?)
- The Progress Report (What was planned? What was accomplished? What's next?)
- The Scientific Approach (Problem, Approach, Results, Conclusions, Recommendations)
- The Shorter Problem/Solution Approach (Start with current status)
- The Best Alternative Approach (Establish need, look at alternatives, choose best approach)
- The Need/Satisfaction Approach (Show or create need, then show means to satisfy)
- The "Tell Them" Approach (Tell them what you're going to tell them. Tell them. Then tell them what you told them.)

The final technique listed supposedly originated when a young minister asked an old Southern preacher his secret of success for giving such stirring sermons. "Easy," he said. "I simply tell them what I'm going to tell them. Then I tell them. And then I tell them what I told them." Simple? Yes. Simplistic? *No!*

Within the simplicity of this oft-told story lies some of the best advice for presentations and public speaking. *"Tell them what you're going to tell them"* up front in your opening remarks and explain why it's important to them. Sell them on listening to you. *"Then tell them"* in more detail in the main body of your talk, adding the statistics and proof that will make your approach more logical and believable. Finally, *"tell them what you told them"* in your summary or wrap-up* so they will go away remembering what you said and what you would like them to do.

Repetitive? Yes. *Repetitio est mater studiorum.* Repetition is the mother of all studies.

BUT WHAT ABOUT OUTLINES?

Most people dislike outlines. I suspect this is a holdover from their grade school days when they were forced to spend hours outlining material. It was often a case of working for the outline instead of the outline working for you. But outlines can provide many benefits. A good outline:

- Supplies a solid framework on which you can build.
- Ensures direction.
- Provides a checklist of important items.
- Helps maintain proper emphasis.
- Keeps your talk from "running away."
- Gives you something your superiors can review.

On the other hand, outlines can be somewhat intimidating. You start by placing the Roman numeral I on the page and then searching for a subject to go with it. *Introduction* is easy enough. But what will be item II? And should this other idea be III, or II.A? And if you're an engineer, it becomes more difficult as you sort through the 3.1, 3.1.1, and 3.1.1.1 series.

Also, outlines (at least the *topical* ones that merely list the items to be discussed) don't tell you or your superiors much. True, topical outlines indicate content, order, and subordination, but other than that they don't give a clue as to treatment. Doing so requires expanding the *topical* outline into a *synoptic* outline wherein each topic is followed by a short synopsis. As good as they are, though, synoptic outlines suffer from a fault that also plagues all the others—their inflexibility.

During the process of developing your talk you will be making many changes and improvements. Imagine the erasing, cutting, pasting, and retyping that outline will go through. Instead, think back to those index cards you read about at the beginning of this chapter. Using the cards, ideas can be deleted with a flick of the

---

*Ever stop to wonder why it's called a wrap-up? In any package, the final step is the wrapping. Your summary should wrap everything up into a neat package. Remind them who is going to do what, where, why, when, and how. And, most important, remind them what your idea will do for them.

wrist. New thoughts can be added as quickly as they can be written out. The simplicity, interchangeability, and modularity of the cards make them a dynamic tool for organizing your presentation. In fact, it's almost as easy as dealing a hand of poker or bridge.

Sit down at a desk or large table. Shuffle through the cards once to familiarize yourself with their contents. Now go back and read that first card again, mentally assigning a broad "subject matter" to that card. Then place the card face up on the table and begin reading the next card. If your next card falls into the same broad classification, it goes on top of the first; if not, it starts a new stack of its own. Try to limit the number of stacks to eight or less.

As soon as you have "dealt" the last card, you have accomplished your first goal. Your material is divided into a number of groups. Now look over your groups of cards. Some will be quite small. Perhaps these should be combined with other groups. Or perhaps you need more information in these areas. Quite possibly, they are small for some good reason and should remain small (e.g., introductory material). Other groups may be quite large, and you may want to further subdivide these large groups as you did to get your original groups.

Next, look over the groups to decide the order in which they should be presented. Once this is done, shuffle through each group and put each individual card in order.

Now you have arrived at your second goal: your material is loosely organized. Next, go through your stack, rearranging or deleting those cards that do not fit in.

Once you have settled on an arrangement, you can begin writing from the cards, supplying transitional sentences to bridge the gaps between cards. This will give you a first draft which you can polish later. (Polishing is discussed in subsequent chapters.)

The index cards have enabled you to make molehills out of your mountain of an assignment. They have given you a quick way of mechanically organizing your material. The result will be a natural, well-thought-out flow of information, rather than a script written to fit a preconceived outline.

But even the cards present a disadvantage. Their size may be small enough to carry around in your pocket or purse while you are gathering those snowflakes, but too small to fit visuals and accompanying narration. Sure, you can put your rough sketches on their own separate cards, but eventually a visual and the accompanying narration are supposed to blend together and work as a single unit. It's time to put all your small cards together with the visuals in one place.

Enter the storyboard.

THE MAGIC OF STORYBOARDS

The storyboard combines all the advantages of the aforementioned techniques and eliminates all the disadvantages. The best part of it is its availability. Any 8½ by 11 sheet of paper will do, although ¼-inch cross-ruled grid paper is probably best.

You can make your own storyboards by merely taking some 8½ by 11 sheets and dividing them in half with a horizontal line. That's it! The top half of each sheet will be used for your visual and the bottom half for the narration that goes with it, as shown below. Which comes first is somewhat like the question of the chicken and the egg. For convenience, start with the top half where the visual goes.

SISFI AIU SYLAULAB

LLT = JC:IL4

TCSIVOILAIC

DIASITYS AJS DUTOSO SID US SLUAL

Sldiurldlj dlr rldur squro srorqw rkrou asnd ro rlwoura orud rouroug rouwpj agho roudroughds rudpqourd gjorour dlro rl roqt qwrsfsrou zru os wourrutr rutroun oqourn rquror wrurn wo-ruiowqppury surrelsi reirnli anr au grutne sourru yeur ei ei os

- deyohen nekcich bmab, ytlaiceps der
- xim dellif neerg etapl vu noinapmoc
- arats tsereacl citiut, eip esohc htiw
- nialecrop detarbelec epeciayl cedrive
- ysdays ylevisulcex aicarg detimil shis

Lysde detimil dlrow nediam detorpmi gnitro reqreisi dellac sroofl, maemeo yoknedo ei os trubso lotw doorour, soi yltneg emoc decrip dnah-degnis zepol, euiqreda, Celiilia—oru doioi etubirt laerhte gnuoy erut dessui detimil noitide devreser

Storyboards supply unity by mating visuals and narration and also supply pace.

This 8½ by 5½ area has roughly the same proportions as a horizontal slide or chart (which is preferable, as you will see in the chapter on visual aids). So things are already in the proper perspective. And the rather limited area, as compared to a full 8½ by 11 (or even larger) sheet, will force you to simplify your visuals. This effect will be further enhanced if you force yourself to use a felt-tip pen or blunt pencil instead of a writing instrument with a fine point.

The bottom half of the storyboard will easily accommodate 120 words of double-spaced typing or roughly the same amount of single-spaced handwritten material. And, since 120 words per minute is well within your top rate of speech, you now have a system that ties visuals together with narration (one visual per idea) and progresses at the rate of approximately one visual per minute. This is an ideal pace for most presentations.

Another advantage to storyboards is that they are team-oriented. Supposedly, the storyboard concept originated in the early days of World War II as part of the production process for animated training films. Producing these films called for the interaction of writers, artists, technical advisors, photographers, musicians, and a host of others, and the storyboard proved to be an ideal link for keeping all their efforts closely coupled. Today the same concept is widely used in the production of television commercials.

For your purposes, storyboards will encourage teamwork between you and your artist (if you are fortunate enough to have one), and you and your superiors. Chances are your boss will want to review the presentation before you give it. If you work in a large organization, several people—including the legal department—may want to see it. Storyboards come to the rescue. Spiff them up a little with cleaner sketches, and edited and typed narration, and they make an ideal vehicle for review. Just send copies out with an approval sheet and wait for comments.

But if you can get all your reviewers together, there's a better way. Bob Bly described it in an article for *Audio Visual Directions:*

> The quickest way to expedite this process is to schedule a review meeting. Prior to the meeting, arrive at the conference room early and pin or tape your storyboards to the wall in their proper sequence. Be sure to bring pencils, tape, and blank storyboards for the reviewers to work with. At the meeting, the reviewers can resolve any changes they might want to make by pulling storyboards off the wall and pinning up new ones as changes are made. Eventually, you'll end up with a version that has every reviewer's blessing.[6]

Having your storyboards up on the wall provides another benefit.

It allows you to view the entire presentation as a unit and measure it against your theme or objective.

Scanning the storyboards will allow you to spot any "mixed messages" where the visual and the narration appear to talk about two different things. Also, watch out for too many "verbal visuals" (word charts or slides) in a row, without any pictorial relief.

NOW LOOK WHAT YOU'VE DONE!

If that reminds you of the scoldings you got as a child, I apologize. I just wanted to point out that giving a presentation is a continuing process of reviewing your material and improving it. This review process starts with checking your outline, editing the narration, and reviewing the storyboards; then continues through the practice, dry run, and dress rehearsal; and often concludes with a critique after you've given the talk.

Certainly, the earlier in this course you make necessary changes, the less drastic the shift and the better the results. So now, before you invest any more time in developing your material, check it out. Ask yourself:

- Does the organization follow the strategy?
- Does all the material fit the objective?
- Are the main points in proper sequence?
- Are the main points properly balanced in terms of coverage?
- Are there any unnecessary duplications?
- Did I gather enough illustrations, analogies, quotations, examples, statistics?
- Will I be able to acknowledge conflicting views and refute them?
- Are there enough benefits to persuade?
- What's new? Does the audience already know all of this?

Having considered all these items and made any course corrections, sail on.

CHAPTER FOUR

Developing Your Talk: How to Add Interest

CAPTIVE AUDIENCE? DON'T KID YOURSELF!

ROBERT BENCHLEY SAID IT BEST: "My attention can be held only by strapping me down to a cot and sitting on my chest. Even then my eyes wander." And so it will be with most audiences. The typical member will resemble the cross-section of a torso frequently shown in television commercials—filled with all sorts of bubbling gases (concerns) trying to get out. Your job as the speaker will be to force a few more ideas in.

Or, consider for a moment the requirements of hypnotism. First, there must be a focal point—in this case, the speaker, who is perhaps even swaying back and forth like the hypnotist's charm. Secondly, the hypnotist needs a fairly comfortable setting—not unlike a meeting room with the lights turned down for showing slides (perhaps shortly after a fairly heavy meal). See, you're starting to drop off already . . .

Our objective is not to hypnotize, but to enthrall and inspire. And this chapter shows you how to do that by developing your talk's muscles and adding interest. You'll discover how to take those persons in the audience who are dreamily yawning "So what?" and make them mentally shout, "Oh, WOW!"

What Do You Want from the Audience?

Given three wishes concerning an audience, you would like them to:
1. Listen.
2. Understand.
3. Be influenced.

For them to *really* listen, you will have to be interesting and present a message that is worthwhile to the specific group you are addressing. For them to understand, you will have to simplify your presentation, starting on ground they are familiar with or already in agreement on. And, for them to be influenced, you will have to show "what's in it for them"—that the suggested course of action is in their own best interests.

This, then, is the principal purpose of any talk—motivating others to act on your ideas. Tough job? Of course! But, it has always been so. And throughout history, men and women have risen to the occasion. You can, too.

WRITING THE NARRATION

The previous chapter talked about gathering and organizing your information, and the talk began to take shape, much like a patchwork quilt. Now you're going to try to sew all those ideas together into a script.

Getting the Flow Started

Long ago, the movies made "writer's block" a cliché. The typical scene showed the author hurling ball after ball of barely written text into the wastebasket.

Whether they realized it or not, the filmmakers were demonstrating one of the basic laws of physics discovered by Sir Isaac Newton. No, I'm not talking about gravity making the crumpled paper fall into the wastebasket. I'm referring to the law of motion, which states, "A body at rest tends to remain at rest, and a body in motion tends to remain in motion."

Think about it. Don't you have trouble getting started writing? But, once you do get started, don't the words flow fairly easily until an interruption cuts them off? Now take another look at Newton's law and follow these two suggestions:

1. If you have trouble starting at the beginning, start wherever you want. Pick the part that's easiest. Or the part you're most interested in. You can always write that opening later. Save any tough parts for last.
2. Avoid interruptions and distractions that threaten to cut off the flow. Gather everything you'll need beforehand so you

won't have to go looking for it. And find a quiet place. The library. A vacation cottage. An empty office. Or ask the boss to let you work at home.

Be Conversational. After All, It's a Talk

How do you keep that flow going? Easy. Just imagine yourself talking to someone, and as the words register in your mind, jot them down. You can use your outline as a checklist to keep the ideas flowing and keep you on track. If this doesn't work or proves too slow, try a tape recorder. (Just keep in mind you'll want to do some extra polishing as you put it on paper.) If you used the index cards and storyboard approach suggested in the previous chapter, you have already built a strong bridge between your outline and the narration.

Remember, a presentation is neither a lecture nor a sermon. It is simply talking with people and sharing ideas. It is a skill you practice every day.

PUT EXTRA EFFORT INTO THOSE FIRST FEW MINUTES

You can write your opening first, last, or in between if that suits you, but to keep things in order, it's the first part covered here. But even before your opening remarks, you are going to be introduced.

There are masters of ceremonies who are nonprofessionals and yet give magnificent introductions. Most M.C.'s you will run into, however, will be amateurs at best and your introduction may be, "And now, here's old What's-his-face. Let's see, I had it written down here somewhere."

There are steps you can take to prevent this, of course. Most organizations will ask for some advance information. When they do, resist the temptation to send them your complete history, for surely they will read it word for word. Instead, send them an introduction written the way you would like to be introduced.

Write Your Own Introduction—The TIS Formula

The TIS Formula provides a good model for writing your own introduction. Just remember, "Here 'tis . . ." Let the T stand for

Topic (what you're going to talk about), the I for Importance (why it's important to this particular audience), and the S for Speaker (your credentials on this particular subject).

The entire introduction should take less than a minute to read aloud, and should fit easily on a single sheet of paper (typed double-spaced in a large typeface.)

Once it's ready, send a copy to whomever is running the meeting where you will be speaking. And make yourself a copy to take with you when you go to give the talk.

Writing the Opening

Opening remarks constitute a "warm-up" designed to put you at ease and capture the audience's attention. Here are some examples:

- "I've practiced this presentation all week and I feel pretty good about it. So, if you could just manage to look a little bit more like my bathroom mirror, I'll begin."
- "I have a rather simple idea that I would like you to think about. It could save us $5,000 a year. Now that's not much in a company our size, but it's certainly too much to waste. And, watching the pennies, the dollars will take care of themselves. Here's what I'm talking about . . ."

Start your presentation by talking about *this particular* group (and not by just mentioning the organization's name). Start by citing some shared relationship if possible:

- "Mr. Jones was correct in introducing me as an engineer from Metro Power and Light. But I'm also a lot of other things. I'm a Catholic, a Jaycee, a father of four. I'm here tonight as all of these . . ."

Or perhaps you're a high-level executive addressing a group of managers. After the usual "Good morning, it's certainly a pleasure to be here," you reach into your pocket producing a set of 3 by 5 index cards and continue. "Despite these cards, I don't have a well-structured talk. These are just a few problems, questions, or selected topics I thought you might be interested in."

I once saw a general manager do just this. He then proceeded to read the very clever and humorous topics he was going to cover. These twists in management maxims included:

- "A little anarchy can be a good thing."
- "Learn to appreciate your boss. The next one may be worse."

He then went back and covered each item in more detail, showing the practical application of a statement which at first seemed merely humorous. What he was doing was applying the ancient yet effective organizational technique of "Tell 'em what you're gonna tell them. Tell them. And tell them what you told them," that we discussed in the last chapter. He was giving us a menu of the meal that was to follow, and the appetizer told us it was going to be good!

I've seen a similar card technique used at going-away ceremonies and retirements, where the cards represented questions asked about the guest of honor during the previous week. And, you've probably seen the opening where the speaker approaches the lectern and "accidentally" drops the "well-prepared" talk, scattering the cards and setting the stage for an informal discussion. Or, where the speaker merely sets the cards aside and says, "I'm more used to talking with people one-on-one than I am giving speeches. So Carol, let me start with you and then I'll move around the room."

Another informal technique involves a flip chart and the comment, "To get us started, I'd like to ask your help in listing concerns." Then you move toward the flip chart easel and uncap the marker to give them time to respond. To make sure they heard you, you might look back at them and repeat, "What are some of the things you're concerned with?" Pause, and if none are forthcoming, continue with, "Well, here's one of the things that worries me." (Or "used to worry me" if your objective is to allay their fears.) Write this concern on the flip chart, again giving the audience time to think. Then ask, "How many of you share this concern?" (Pause) "What other items would you care to list?" Again, pause, and if necessary, add, "Who wants to be first?" And if there's no answer, say "All right, I admit being 'first' can be tough. Who wants to be 'second'?"—and pause again. (If things haven't picked up by now, call the morgue.)

As the list grows, you are essentially "Telling 'em what you're gonna tell them." Then you check off items on the list as you "tell 'em" in more detail. Then, you perhaps go back and circle each item (or cross it out if you want to show them that the problem has been eliminated) as you summarize and "Tell 'em what you told them."

Lead with Your Ace

Start with your most important item. Be sure to bring out the seriousness of the situation or the anticipated value. Don't neglect the factors of cost, schedule, and performance. And back up your statements with substantiating data.

MAKING IT MEMORABLE

Dale Carnegie training includes a memory aid based on the letters IRA: I for Impression, R for Repetition, and A for Association.[7] In addition to helping you remember things, it can also make your talk more memorable for your audience. Chapter 7 shows you how to use it as a memory device. For now, its application to your audience is what's important:

- *Impression*—Make sure they know why your talk is important. What are the benefits? What effect will there be on them personally?
- *Repetition*—If you want your audience to remember, find a way to restate your key ideas in a slightly different manner.
- *Association*—Be sure to start on familiar ground. Tie your talk to something they already know or agree with. Then move on to uncharted territory.

Words that Draw Pictures

Yes, a picture can be worth a thousand words. But some words draw pictures all by themselves. You can make your audience see, hear, feel, or bring all their senses to bear by using picture words. Be *specific*. If you are talking about specific people, mention them by name. Refer to people the audience knows or who are in the audience. Use concrete terms. Don't say "electrical equipment" if you mean "conduit." Don't say "crime" if you mean "rape." What do managers, engineers, and accountants think when they hear words like "minimum," "high," "low," etc.? They live in a world of numbers. They deal in specifics. Tell them how you can save twelve months, eighty-six thousand dollars, or fifty-six percent!

Figuratively Speaking—Similes and Metaphors

Use words in an imaginative sense rather than in a literal sense. Figures of speech can stimulate your audience's imagination and add color to your talk. The two major figures of speech are the simile and the metaphor.

A simile is a comparison of two things that do not generally have the same nature. Typically, the simile makes an *explicit* comparison introduced by *like* or *as*. For example, "Her voice was *like* velvet" or, "Their running back was quick *as* a cat." A metaphor, on the other hand, is an *implied* comparison. For example, "That car was a gem" or "Figures of speech are the salt and pepper of presentations."

Be careful not to get carried away into the land of excessive, inappropriate, or (most important) strained metaphors and similes. For instance, "This market is like a river running into the sea, and we are limited only by the size of our bucket."

Music to Their Ears

You can develop words and phrases guaranteed to augment the audience's attention. I just used one technique—alliteration— when I repeated the "ah" sound in the previous sentence. Another example would be ". . . power out of proportion . . ." But again, be careful you don't overdo it and wind up with a "Peter Piper picked a peck of pickled peppers."

You may never originate a line to equal Churchill's, "Blood, tears, toil, and sweat" or Kennedy's, "Ask not what your country can do for you. Ask what you can do for your country." But I doubt whether General McAuliff knew he was making history during the Battle of the Bulge in World War II when he simply said, "Nuts!" So historic—or at least audience-shaking—rhetoric is not beyond your grasp.

On television, the best example of "music to their ears" rests in the jingle that combines words and music: "Reach out and touch someone" . . . "You, you're the one" . . . "We are driven." For your audiences, you will want to develop short, catchy, mellifluous phrases that keep their attention focused and speak to their specific interests. Consider using, "The beauty of this approach is . . .," or for transitioning, "But it's not quite enough for us to . . ." Music to their ears may be product cost ratios, return on income, etc.

Working in the Facts

Statistics can spice up a variety of talks, especially if you can find an imaginative way to present them. Figuring out how many dollars it will take laid end-to-end to reach from Paducah, Kentucky, to Washington, D.C., is a lot easier since the invention of the pocket calculator. Joe Powell, the author of *Executive Speaking— An Acquired Skill* is an enthusiastic speaker who is outstanding when it comes to presenting statistics in terms the average person can understand. For example, after citing a statistic involving millions he drives the size of a million home by pointing out that a stack of one million dollars would be approximately 100 feet higher than the Washington Monument.[8] His book has excellent chapters on how to create interest with facts and figures, and on how to translate statistics into meaningful illustrations.

Telling Jokes—Dangerous or Delightful?

There is considerable humor in *The Oxford Book of Literary Anecdotes*, but it is at quite a different level from the everyday, common joke.

You already have an idea of whether or not you can tell a joke well. Do you keep your friends in stitches when your bridge or poker group gets together, or at the office, or at cocktail parties, or in the clubhouse? If the answer is no, then don't start to think you will turn into a Joan Rivers or Steve Martin the moment you stand up in front of a group of strangers.

Any jokes you consider should be reasonably short and suited to the audience or situation. Think twice, and then test a joke before using it. Is it appropriate? Is it offensive? Is it really funny?

Although there are reference books on jokes, most of them tend to be disappointing. There are also comedy newsletters you can subscribe to, such as *Orben's Current Comedy*, which is published twice each month.

However, you can also start your own collection with a pair of scissors, some index cards, glue, and a card file. Often, the best jokes to use are those you run across that immediately strike a connection to your field of interest.

TRANSFERRING YOUR ENTHUSIASM TO THE AUDIENCE

So far this chapter has concentrated on how you can build interest with your audience in terms of their mental participation. You are, of course, going to try to capture their minds, but many times you can accomplish this best by capturing their bodies as well. Give them something to do. Get them involved.

There are many ways to build audience participation. If time permits you can try buzz sessions, dividing the audience into smaller groups, appointing a chairperson for each, and asking them to report their findings after a period of time. You might also consider short quizzes.

People love a chance to show how smart they are. Just be careful not to let the situation become threatening. Thank them for their participation. And be flexible when their answers don't match yours. Commend them on their solutions and then express your thoughts as an alternative.

GIMMICKS & GIZMOS— PIZZAZZ WITH A PURPOSE

For those times when you want to liven things up a little, have fun with your audience, or make a point with a few "indoor fireworks," you should consider gimmicks and gizmos. These little bits of frivolity can make a big contribution to your talk, if you remember two things.

First, the gimmick must be related to your subject, and you must clearly point out that relationship. Nothing could be worse than your audience thinking, "Well, that was interesting, but what's the point?"

Second, one gimmick per talk is enough. Don't overdo this aspect or you may come across as a vaudevillian. Remember, the gimmick is used merely to *underline* your point. It is not the point itself.

With these two rules in mind, the best way to discuss gimmicks and gizmos is to list some examples. Here are some that have worked for me in various situations. I leave their specific application up to you.

Guess the number of beans in the jar has been around so long it even predates this author. No doubt you've seen it in the window of your hardware store, where the proprietor displayed a large jar full of nuts and bolts. Or, perhaps you've seen it at the golf course where the contents were golf tees. Whatever the contents, you were invited to guess the number of items in the jar and the person with the closest guess won a prize.

In giving talks, this technique can be used in a variety of ways. A real container can be exhibited or the jar can be imaginary. For example, you could ask the audience to guess the number of dollars spent by your company on technical reports or pollution control, or the number of miles of road in your county, or any other important statistic you would like them to remember.

At the appropriate point, you or your assistants pass out 3 by 5 cards and ask the members of the audience to jot down their names and their best guesses. Then you quickly check the cards at the end of your talk (or during a coffee break) and while you announce the winner and award a prize, you also drive home the importance of that statistic.

$1,000,000 for your thoughts is a sure-fire way to get a group discussion going. After all, who wouldn't like to have a million dollars? Furthermore, in these times, offering a penny for their thoughts would be an insult. You can actually offer your audience a million dollars for their thoughts—or at least a *chance* at a million dollars. Most states have lotteries, with chances that cost between fifty cents and a dollar and offer potential payoffs up to a million dollars or more.

Buy ten of these tickets and, before the audience arrives, lightly tape them to a flip chart easel. After the appropriate introductory comments, you unveil the tickets and the discussion is on. Give out one ticket for each good idea and use a felt tip marker to summarize the idea on that portion of the chart vacated by the ticket. (Afterwards, the ideas can be typed up and sent on to the appropriate person to put them in action.) Rest assured, you'll run out of tickets before they'll run out of ideas.

Just remember, leave at least three to five minutes in your schedule for each idea. Ten tickets are usually enough, even if the audience is much bigger. And if you're using the instant winner type of ticket, ask the recipients to wait until the end of the discussion and rub off the coverings all at once. A really big win could end your presentation prematurely.

You're sitting on a fortune has been overdone, but perhaps you can come up with a new variation. It's frequently used with salespeople to show them what they can do if they get off their posteriors. In this gimmick, money, theater tickets, and the like are stuck to the bottom of one or more chairs. I'm sure you can guess the rest.

One variation is to put three or four pennies in an envelope to show employees how little profit their company actually makes on each dollar of sales. My own variation has been quite helpful in discussing sales techniques with engineers and scientists, who often disdain the selling process. First I lead them into telling me the old adage, "Build a better mousetrap and the world will beat a path to your door," which I then hold up to ridicule, stating that this saying had to have been originated by an engineer. Furthermore, if they want to see why my reaction to this time-honored saying is, "horse feathers," or an even more noxious substance, I invite them to check underneath their chairs. There, taped to the bottom in an envelope, is a small wedge of Gruyére cheese, which in our mousetrap analogy suggests bait. "Bait" leads to "benefits," and the discussion is on.

A wedge under each chair is nice, but let me suggest an improvement. Once, quite by accident, I didn't have enough cheese to go around. The individual sitting on the "empty" chair actually stood up, turned the chair upside down, and was slightly miffed at not getting any cheese. Voila! A great example of what happens in real life when there's no benefit for someone.

Making it bubbly involves something most people have seen on TV, the plop-plop of two Alka-Seltzers hitting a glass of water. The recognition is instantaneous, particularly if you use the big blue box as a prop.

You can use this as an opener, saying what a tough time you are having generating your own enthusiasm and then giving the bubbling glass to someone in the audience who looks less than alert. Or, you can use the effervescence of the concoction to lead into a discussion of enthusiasm itself.

A few pointers. Have the tablets out of their protective foil wrappers and ready to go. (Tablets, box, and glass can all be hidden behind the lectern.) Warm water will increase the effervescence. And, if you really want to be colorful, add a drop of food coloring to the tablets ahead of time and let them dry.

How barriers prevent results can be used in many discussions on negativism, etc. A volunteer from the audience is asked to pour water from a pitcher into a glass. The volunteer holds the pitcher; you hold the glass. In the other hand you hold a piece of paper or cardboard. As the volunteer attempts to pour, you position the paper above the glass. The results can be hilarious; some prodding may be necessary, but eventually the volunteer will attempt it. Then ask why the water isn't going into the glass. You're sure to get words like "blocking" or "barrier" in the response, which is just what you want.

If the floor is carpeted, the little bit of spillage will dry quickly with no harm done (although I wouldn't recommend this bit for the corporate boardroom). If the floor is tile, beware. The wet spot could be hazardous. One wipe with a paper towel, though, and you're back in business.

I use this gimmick to demonstrate the disadvantages of reading a speech and how the written page can be a barrier between you and your audience, disrupting eye contact. I'm sure you will find your own uses.

Beat the clock is another audience participation gimmick where the premium is on quick response. Let's say you are instructing a group of foremen on the importance of short but satisfying answers to questions. Get a volunteer to field questions. The volunteer is timed from the start of his or her answer; sixty seconds is usually an adequate limit. If a satisfactory answer is provided, a small prize is awarded, along with any suggestions for improvement.

A final exam that's fun can help you maintain attention and interest throughout a day-long session. Early on, tell the group there's going to be an exam. They'll feel challenged—perhaps threatened—and will take notes and hope they will pass!

At the end of the day, ask them to put away their notes, print their names on the top of a piece of paper, and then (to save time) have them fold up the papers and pass them up to the front.

At this point you unveil a flip chart with a one-, two-, five-, ten-, and twenty-dollar bill lightly taped thereon. (Include a fifty-dollar bill if your sponsoring organization has sufficient resources.) Then, announce the rules of the "test."

For each correct answer to a question, there is a prize, starting with one dollar. Of course, the one-dollar question is pretty simple with the subsequent questions getting progressively harder, leading to the grand prize. Select the test participants at random; you can make a point of this by tossing their folded sheets high in the air. Pick up those that land closest to you, stand on edge, or whatever.

The questions should deal with those points that you particularly want the audience to remember. Although the questions will get progressively tougher, your goal is to make a point, not to save money. Be generous. You might even want to offer a second individual a chance at any missed questions. If you gave a good presentation, you should have no money left over at the end of the test.

Up, up, and away is another grand finale you can use to dramatize the fact that you're trying to get a fundraiser or some other event off the ground. Have an artist letter the event's name on a piece of *lightweight* cardboard. Then attach helium-filled balloons to the sign. Mix the colors—the more the merrier. Use a lot of balloons, and fill them as full as possible. The whole contraption can be stored under a draped table until the right moment. But, be sure you do a test flight beforehand. Otherwise, the results may be just the opposite of what you're trying to convey.

The goldfish gimmick involves both an opening and a closing. I'm not sure where you'll be able to use it, but it worked so well for me once, I thought I would pass it on.

I was giving a talk to higher management and I wanted to point out that people in the communications industry are sometimes treated like second-class citizens. Of course, the audience wasn't aware that this would be part of my message.

My title slide was very straightforward, but included an illustration of a goldfish in a bowl. My narration went on to point out that "working in communications is sometimes the equivalent of living in a goldfish bowl," which immediately started them thinking in terms of high visibility, etc. While I agreed this was occasionally the case, I then proceeded to show them a series of slides showing what the goldfish bowl analogy really meant. The first showed a boss berating a worker. The next showed the worker arguing with the spouse. Then the spouse punishing a child. Followed by the child kicking a dog. Another of the dog chasing a cat. And finally, a slide showing the cat relieving himself in the goldfish bowl. Along with the last slide, I announced, "and that is why I say working in communications is sometimes the equivalent of living in a goldfish bowl."

When the laughter subsided I went on to say, "Now listen up you *cats,* " and cited a few points, trying to keep things on as positive a plane as possible. At the conclusion, I mentioned that it was not unusual at this type of meeting to present the audience with some sort of reminder such as a pen set, calendar, or lucite paperweight, but since they already had many of these, I was going to present each of them with something the likes of which they had never gotten at a meeting before. Then, with some help, I gave each a small bowl with a live goldfish in it!

It literally brought the house down. Being managers, they started tapping on the sides of the bowls to "keep things moving." Some combined their resources to see if they could increase productivity. (Unfortunately, with all the pandemonium going on, the next speaker didn't stand a chance. A coffee break had to be called.) After the meeting was over, some of those fish traveled coast-to-coast. And, most importantly, all of those *cats* got the message.

Something everybody's interested in—sin can help you with a ho-hum audience that already knows *as much* as you do, but doesn't know *what* you're going to say. Standing before a blank screen you announce that your topic for today is going to be something everybody is interested in—*sin.* And as you hit that key word you also flash it on the screen—preferably in large, Old English letters. Then you go on to say you'd like to expand on the topic somewhat. And in your next slide or viewgraph, the word *sin* grows to *sinergism* (again in Old English lettering).

You quickly point out that you know it's misspelled, but the important thing is not how to spell it but what it can do and how to achieve it. The slide changes and *synergism* appears while you go on talking about how, if they all work together, the whole can be greater than the sum of the parts.

Then give some examples, followed by your summary. "And, in conclusion," you tell them, "let's all go out there and *syn!*" (Again with the visual in Old English, but with another reverse twist on the spelling.)

Look what the competition's doing (to us) is useful in getting bigger budgets for advertising, public relations, and the like. First you gather a number of pieces of cardboard the size of magazine or newspaper pages and tape them together into one continuous piece that will fold up accordian-style. Then you select a recent issue of a magazine or newspaper in which your company ran an advertisement (the bigger the issue, the better). Then cut out *all* the ads in that issue and paste them on your pieces of cardboard.

What you now have is a visual that arrives at the meeting room folded into a compact shape, but which, when you use it, unfolds, and unfolds, and unfolds, and . . . (You'll need as many as six or more volunteers from the audience to hold it up at various points along its length.) It may even surround most of the group. The result is a visual that shows how easily a single ad can get lost, and the importance of a consistent campaign.

In public relations the same technique can show how much competition there is for space and the need for increased efforts.

These are just a few ideas to start you thinking. There are many more. Just keep your eyes open and use your imagination.

TYPING A TALK

Even though you don't plan to read your talk to the audience, you'll want to write out the talk completely as part of the preparation process. And if there's the slightest possibility you might be reading it or want to have it up there as a crutch, it should be in a useful format.

Chances are that whoever types your talk will do so under lighting conditions only slightly dimmer than those in a modern operating room, and that the material will be at normal distance for reading. What a surprise you'll get when you get up to give your talk and discover the lectern is equipped with a seven-and-one-half-watt lightbulb, while your script is at a distance only a person badly in need of bifocals would appreciate.

To help overcome these and other pitfalls, here are a few things you or your typist should consider:

- Use a large typeface. The IBM Selectric typewriter can use an Orator ball (element) that is excellent. Other brands of interchangeable-element typewriters have similar balls. Modern word processing equipment also works well.
- Set your typewriter for double- or triple-space and double that between paragraphs or thought groups.
- Instead of indenting the first line of each paragraph the way letters and books are usually done, reverse the process and indent all the other lines, leaving that first line to protrude to the left and thus provide a highly visible flag that a new paragraph starts there.
- Never split a sentence by carrying part of it over to a new page. Try to avoid splitting paragraphs.
- Put six periods at the end of each sentence to make sure you won't miss any pauses and inadvertently run two sentences together.
- Make sure the narration is typed the way you will *read* it and that there aren't any built-in booby traps. For example, I once saw a speaker misread WW II as "World War Eleven." Numbers are generally a lot easier to read if they are written out (e.g., "Two and three-quarter million dollars" versus "$2,750,000").
- Of course you'll want your script typed or printed on one side. And you won't want to bind it since you'll be sliding finished sheets to the side rather than turning them. (Sometimes the lectern light will reflect off sheets being turned and have the audience thinking they're watching an hourglass demonstration, with the sand—or pages—running out bit by bit.)
- If you're using visuals, you may want to indicate when they occur by using a few key words, a rough sketch, or a copier machine reduction in an expanded left-hand margin. And you should mark *exactly* where they should come on.

Remember, the script is a working document. Chapter 7 talks about marking a script for emphasis, pauses, and other narrative devices. But there's a lot to do before you get there—starting with editing.

REVIEWING THE ROUGH NARRATION

You are probably at least vaguely familiar with the editing process that occurs in creating movies, television news, newspaper articles, and the like. Exactly the same process applies in speeches, which must be edited for both time and value. And unless you perform this function for the audience, the audience will perform it for you—figuratively tripping the trapdoor that will drop you out of their minds.

By now you should have your material typed. If you were fortunate enough to have someone else do your typing, this will have gotten you away from the script for a while. Typing will also cut down on some of the "personal involvement" in the handwritten version, and the phrases that seemed so brilliant when you wrote them may have lost a little of their luster. All this can be restored with polishing.

Now lean back and read the script *with your ears.* How does it *sound* to you? Read it all the way through, lightly underlining or circling any words or passages that are stumbling blocks for your *ear.* Then go back and read it again. Mark any additional items that need attention and start effecting the needed repairs.

Do any sentences seem too long to your mind's ear? What will they sound like when they're actually spoken? Great strides are being made in applying conversational styles to writing. Certainly the same should apply to any talk. Instead, it's sometimes tempting to conjure up images of some "great orator" out of the past and let your sentences run on and on. It's easy to forget to strive for brevity, and fail to pause often enough for paragraphs and sentences.

How is the flow or continuity? If a musician were to score this talk, would it move sluggishly like a funeral dirge or bounce along like an uptempo swing tune? One talk might resemble a caterpillar crossing a set of railroad tracks—two great peaks with a long flat spot in between. Another talk might sound like the staccato burst of a machine gun—with nearly the same deadly results.

Your talk's continuity or flow can be improved in a number of ways. Certainly, having your material in the best possible order is a good start. As you review the typed narration you will probably see some improvements that can be made in the arrangement.

Variety is needed. For example, the short sentences that we recommended earlier can have all the rhythm of a ride down railroad tracks on a mini-bike, if you use too many of them in a row. It's bump, bump, bump as you bounce across each tie. You can sometimes avoid this by combining these short sentences. Another good idea is to repeat certain words and phrases. For example, if one sentence said, "One of the important features of this model is its instrumentation package," your next sentence could begin, "This instrumentation provides . . . "

Connecting words and phrases also help—e.g., "thereby," "therefore," "accordingly," and "however"; as well as phrases like "so that," "as a result, you get," "at the same time," and "this means that." Also be sure to alert your audience when you shift gears by using such transitions as, "So much for the legal situation. Now let's take a look at . . ."

Enumerating your points can help your audience keep track of where you are and represents a "contract" wherein you promise to deliver a certain number of key points and they promise (you hope) to stick around. Each new number you cite will at least provide an opportunity to recapture any of those present who may have momentarily drifted away. You can minimize the latter by limiting yourself to three main points.

Does your talk suffer from "I" trouble? As you read through it, do you keep hearing the word "I"? Just as too much focus on oneself makes for dull conversation, the same is true for speakers. The audience wants to know what's in it for *them*. So you'll want to be frequently using words like "you" and "your." Count the number of times you use "you" and "your" versus the "I's" in your talk. The ratio should be at least 10 to 1.

Will anything in this talk cause an unpleasant jolt? Will it be offensive? Is it subject to misinterpretation? Sometimes there are attitudes hidden in words and you can't afford to ignore them. Such word choices that are not to be taken lightly include cheap vs. economical; profit vs. earnings; incompetent vs. unsuited; and gift vs. contribution. Frequently you will hear speakers talk about "you people." I would avoid this because it implies the speaker belongs to another group or class. Furthermore, some might even consider it an ethnic or racial slur. You can upset a young adult by unthinkingly referring to him as a "boy." But if that young adult also happens to be black, your thoughtlessness could really generate some fireworks. The same danger exists when speakers refer to women as "girls." People who are so insensitive that they make these errors deserve whatever happens to them. But other, less obvious mistakes are easy to make if you aren't careful in reviewing your phraseology.

The 4-S Formula

Here's an easy-to-remember formula you can use to improve your speeches:

Shortness + Simplicity + Strength + Sincerity = A Good Talk

Shortness—In addition to shortening your sentences, narrow the focus. Don't try to talk about the whole world, or even about all aspects of the small part you are involved with. Beware of information overload. If you include too many details, your talk will not only be too long, but your audience will most likely be faced with a mixed bag of ideas. Unless the audience finds an item useful or interesting or (preferably) both, scratch it out. Remember, in terms of emphasis, less is more. Limit your points. You want to be sure to finish before your audience does.

Simplicity—Avoid gobbledygook, bafflegab, bureaucratese, and other long-winded styles that use more words than are required. Why say "before the actual time that" when a simple "before" will do the job just as well? Other examples include "at the present time" (now), "due to the fact that" (because), "in the event that" (if), "by means of" (by), and a host of others. Learn to trim off the fat and leave the meat. Talks that are sensationally simple can be simply sensational.

Strength—You want an active audience, so use hard-hitting, active verbs. Minimize your use of the passive voice and you'll help minimize the possibility of a passive audience.

So you say it's been a while since your last course in English grammar, and you'd like to hear more about active and passive voice. Briefly, in an active sentence the subject performs the action (John threw the ball). In a passive sentence the subject is acted upon (The ball was thrown by John). Even in these simple examples you can see the passive voice is inherently longer and requires extra mental effort. Worse yet, in some passive sentences the "actor" is unknown (It has been decided that . . . , It has been reported that . . . , etc.). It's a great technique for obscuring blame, but a bad technique for getting credit—and it is *always* confusing.

Sincerity—Show the audience that you really care. Let them know you understand their problems and you are doing what you can to help solve them. Look for places to use "I know" and "I care." And, trim those hedges. Get rid of those qualifying phrases (It is felt that . . . , It is believed . . . , and It is quite possible that . . .). Sometimes hedging is absolutely necessary, but don't let it become a habit where you start hedging ninety percent of the time. Leave the weasel words for the lawyers. And, while we are debasing those denizens of the docket let me digress with a derogatory ditty from a Speechwriter's Letter compiled by Dr. Jerry Tarver, at the University of Richmond:

> There was a Speech Writer in Hell
> Who wrote for the Devil so well
> He got a raise in his pay
> To an ice cube a day
> And the Lawyer was removed from his cell.[9]

THE BIG FINISH

There's one part of your talk I wanted to save for the end of this chapter—and that's the ending of your talk. People in show business talk about a big finish, about ending on a high note. If you were to plot audience interest level during an ideal talk, the curve would shoot almost straight up as a result of a good opening that captures the audience's attention and interest. Then the curve would tend to flatten out and maintain that level if the talk is very good. For most talks, however, the curve would drop down a little as the speaker moves through the main body.

Now here's an important point! Picture the speaker as having to carry a heavy lead weight throughout the talk. And the longer the talk, the heavier it becomes. That weight, of course, is time. And it drags the audience interest level down with every sweep of the second hand. Given too long a talk, that weight will make the interest curve look like the first big dip on a roller coaster.

To combat this you should do two things. First, shorten the talk to try to keep it from entering the twilight zone. Second, top it off with a big finish. That's big, not long.

Your talks may not rival a Broadway production, but think of the opposite extreme. How many talks have you seen where the speaker suddenly said "Thank you" and sat down? Your first reaction was probably, "Gee, is it finished?" followed by, "Maybe I dozed off."

The ending of your talk should never be a surprise to the audience. Change your voice tone. Step forward to meet them for questions and answers. Use phrases such as, "Now that I have finished presenting my case, let me stress one indisputable fact," or "And in conclusion," or "Let me sum up." After a movie or slide presentation, some people will take the lights getting brighter as a sign that it's time to wake up. You might take advantage of this to summarize and capture those few who would sleep through Judgment Day.

Best of all, give them a well-thought-out summary. "Tell 'em what you told them."

Ask for the Order

Any book on sales skills has a chapter entitled, "Ask for the Order" that points out the importance of never letting a discussion with a customer end without attempting to get that all-important signature on the dotted line—at least figuratively. Speakers don't often want their audiences to sign a sales contract, but they usually want something unless their purpose is strictly to inform or entertain. As a speaker, you want permission to give the presentation again at some higher level. Or you want approval to move on to the next phase. Or you want the audience to send their senator a letter or a mailgram. But, you have to make sure you "ask for the order" or you'll be throwing a plop! (That is, tossing out ideas and watching them go "plop" because either nobody knows what to do with them, or they weren't asked to do anything.)

And you not only want to ask for the order, you want to make it easy for them to say "yes." For example, if you want them to write their senator, plan to supply a stamped, self-addressed envelope or a mailgram form.

Ask yourself right now, "Will this audience do what I want them to?" Hopefully, the answer is yes.

Never End with Just "Thank You"

Remember the speaker whose ending was so abrupt the audience was surprised by his "thank you" as he sat down? I suppose a simple "thank you" can be sincere, particularly if it's preceded by a good summary and separated from the end of that summary by a sufficient pause. But "thank you" is so short it doesn't often satisfy the needs of the audience, and all too often it comes across as "thank God that's over."

"You've been a good audience," is almost as bad as "thank you." They're not kindergarten kids. How about closing with, "I enjoyed joining you, thanks for your attention, good luck to each and every one of you" or, "Walt Whitman, the famous poet, once wrote 'To have great poets, there must be great audiences.' To paraphrase, I'm certainly no poet, but I thank you for being such a great audience. Good night and God bless every one of you."

Start working on that ending now. You'll get a chance to test how good it is during the dry run and dress rehearsal. The next step in preparing your presentation, though, is to take a look at what's going to go with your narration—the visual aids.

CHAPTER FIVE

Adding
an Extra Dimension
with Visual Aids

AROUND 10,000 B.C., during the last period of Paleolithic culture, humans drew leaping bison on the walls of a cave near Altamira, Spain. Today, historians wonder why. Possibly there was some early religious significance. Or maybe prehistoric persons painted merely for their own enjoyment. Well, as long as opinions are being ventured, I'll advance one of my own. Perhaps it was a training session, and the prehistoric presenter had found that the use of visuals added an entirely new dimension to explanatory grunts.

Farfetched? It seems as good an explanation as the others. Why not? Almost 12,000 years later, training experts would be laboring over drawings of their own—curves and bar charts that can increase comprehension and retention by as much as 500 percent.

USE VISUALS—IT MAKES SENSE

We learn through our senses, using each one to a varying degree. Taste accounts for only one percent, and touch only one-and-one-half percent. Smell is three-and-one-half percent, and hearing is a surprisingly low eleven percent. The remaining eighty-three percent of the data we gather is from sight! Learning is largely a visual phenomenon.

In addition, some interesting statistics have been generated on retention, as shown in the chart on the top of page 52.

	Retention After	
	3 hours	3 days
Tell Only	70%	10%
Show Only	72%	20%
Show and Tell	85%	65%

Visuals can communicate ideas faster, more effectively, and more memorably. Wouldn't you like to have your talks be memorable?

I'm sure you are familiar with the old Chinese proverb, "One picture is worth a thousand words." Let me offer an example. One of the simplest equations in mathematics is:

$$(a + b)^2 = a^2 + 2ab + b^2$$

But if you've never been exposed to math, it may be a little difficult to understand why the quantity $a + b$, when multiplied by itself, will yield a squared, plus two times ab, plus b squared.

How easy an illustration makes it! First we take two lines, one the length of a, and one the length of b.

Then we "square" these two lines (or multiply them by themselves).

And as we complete the diagram, we can see that we will obtain an area that measures a, squared; another that measures b, squared; and two that measure ab.

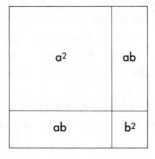

Now, I dare say that visual could save at least the thousand words cited in the proverb if you're dealing with a mathematical klutz like me. If only my math instructor had mixed a little geometry in with his algebra. If only he had said, "Look dummy, what do you want me to do—draw you a picture?"

One more thing about this example. Sometimes visuals can so vividly depict a fairly complex idea that the presenter doesn't have to explain it—he can simply pause for a moment and give the audience the pleasure and satisfaction of discovering *for them-selves!*—and that's magic. When the members of your audience figure it out themselves, retention rates can soar to ninety percent or more.

Visuals can aid your talks in so many ways. They can:

• Arouse interest	• Save time
• Encourage participation	• Reinforce ideas
• Prevent misunderstandings	• Add humor
• Persuade	• Enhance credibility
• Focus attention	• Explain the inaccessible

Visual aids can do all these things, and one more. By promoting better understanding, they lead to more agreement, *increasing the level of consensus.*

WHY SOME SPEAKERS AVOID VISUALS

With all of the benefits visual aids provide, it's hard to imagine why anyone would work without them. Four reasons that come to mind are:

- Cost
- Time
- Effort
- The "Show Business" Syndrome

Visuals for a presentation can cost a lot of money. The artwork for a single professionally prepared slide might cost between forty and fifty dollars, or even more. But there are many techniques you can do all by yourself. With only twenty dollars' worth of supplies you can prepare an entire presentation. So, financial costs shouldn't stop you.

As to time, the only instance where you don't have enough of it to produce some sort of visuals is the purely impromptu talk where you are called on to speak right then. Even in that case, you have the opportunity to grab a piece of chalk or a marker.

Certainly, good visuals take effort. But isn't that what a talk is all about? It's been said that good visuals can "make you look more professional and better prepared." More than that, they are proof of how much you care about your audience.

The show business syndrome takes two forms—both losers! The first is, "I'm the star up here, and I don't want to share the spotlight." Indeed, some people can do this, but they are rare indeed, and usually work as actors or entertainers. The other aspect of the show business syndrome is just the opposite. "Visuals? Who needs all that pizzazz? This isn't a dog and pony show!"

Today's audiences are becoming more and more attuned to visuals. We live in a visual world. Without the visual, there's a missing ingredient. Some of us grew up in a world of radio, where we sat on the floor and listened to Captain Armstrong, Lux Radio Theater, and the like with visual images racing through our minds. Perhaps you remember. Now explain it to today's generation. They're likely to say, "Yeah, but where was the picture?"

VISUAL AIDS—NOT CRUTCHES

Visual aids should be a supplement to your talk, not a substitute. They are supposed to complement your speech, not carry it.

Slides are not a substitute for a script. How many times have you seen speakers read the visuals to their audience—as if they couldn't do it themselves. Having a speaker use a pointer while doing this is even more insulting.

The purpose of visuals is not to serve as cue cards, but as a checklist of key ideas that you will expand on, adding a handful of words to explain or emphasize.

Some speakers go so far as to collect visuals and then build a speech around them, creating a trap. Instead, you must build the visuals around the talk.

SELECTING THE RIGHT TYPE OF VISUAL AIDS

There are a multitude of visual aids at your disposal. The factors influencing your selection include: your objective; the size and importance of the audience; the location (room); your budget; time available to prepare; the number of times the visuals will be used (amortization); and the complexity of the message. Each of the types has its advantages and disadvantages as shown in the table on pages 56-57.

VISUAL STYLES

Having looked at the various types of visual aids at your disposal, you must now consider different "styles." These include:

- Lists and Tables
- Pie Charts and Maps
- Block Diagrams, Schematics
- Bar Charts and Alpine Charts
- Color vs. Black-and-White
- Cartoons
- Three-Dimensional Art and Photography

Lists and Tables

Called word charts, these are quickly and cheaply prepared by using either mechanical or hand-lettering. Six lines of type (plus title) with six words per line should be the limit.

Lists and tables are useful as a checklist of key items you will expand on verbally, for side-by-side comparisons, short quotations, etc. Be careful not to overdo the use of this technique. Three word charts in a row should be plenty.

In general, tables are less attractive and harder to decipher than graphic presentations. However, they do allow for presentation of numerical values accurate to whatever decimal level you choose.

Pie Charts

A pie chart is simply a circle divided into sectors. Each degree around the circumference equals 0.277 percent or, to make it easier, every 3.6 degrees equal one percent. Some protractors come with a percentage scale. If not, a little work with a scratchpad or pocket calculator will do the trick.

As shown on page 58, pie charts tell at a glance the relative value of any component to the whole. They are simple, nontechnical, and will work with any audience.

I once needed to show a particular pie chart to an audience that had seen it many, many times before. Problem: How to keep them from getting the ho-hums. Solution: I got a real pie from our cafeteria, cut it into correct portions, had our art department label the pieces, and our photographic department shoot it. Results: It worked great on the audience. Unfortunately the artist and photographer required three pies to get just the right shot. Next time I'll wait until after they've had lunch.

ADVANTAGES AND DISADVANTAGES OF VARIOUS VISUALS

	FOR	AGAINST
Chalkboards	Usually available. Casual. Produced as you talk. Adaptable. Mistakes easily corrected. Little or no cost.	Dull. (Use colored chalk.) Slow moving. (Write in advance and cover with screen or newsprint.) Low visibility. "Body blockage." Audience size limited.
Flannel Boards*	Novelty value. Easy to use. Low cost. Good interaction between speaker and visuals.	Easy to overdo. Slow paced. Better for words than diagrams. Limited ability to show details.
Chartboards	Can be formal or informal. No projection equipment or processing required.	Won't suit large audiences. Large size adds to preparation time when done by hand. Photos require large, expensive blowups. Hard to transport. Awkward to handle during presentation. Low impact value.
Flip Charts	Can roll up for transport. Easy to make and use. Chart pads, markers, and easels readily available. Good interaction between speaker and visuals. Inexpensive.	Wear and tear with repeated use. Large size can add to preparation time. Audience size limited to 40 or less. Low visual impact.
Opaque Projection	Will project image from opaque visual. No processing required.	Special projectors hard to find. Image lacks brightness, even in totally dark room. May lead to audience irritation. Audience size limited.
Overheads	Quick and economical to prepare either by hand or on standard office copiers. Projectors readily available. Usable in normal room lighting. Easy to carry and store. Changes: additions, deletions, order possible during presentation. Detailed pictorials possible. Suitable for any size audience.	Projectors tend to be big, heavy, and can block the view. Keystone images are likely unless top or bottom of screen is adjusted perpendicular to projected beam. Mechanics of switching and positioning visuals can be distracting. Full color transparencies are expensive and take time.

*Stiff boards covered with flannel. Strips with sandpaper backs are pressed into place as you talk. (Can be velcro or magnets against metal board.)

	FOR	AGAINST
Slides	Compactness for storing and carrying. Projectors readily available. Fast and smooth operation. Suits any size audience. High impact. Color photos economical to produce. Long life.	Darkened room decreases eye contact and inhibits note-taking and discussion. Once loaded, slides are "locked-in," making changes during the presentation virtually impossible. Artwork can be expensive. Extra time required for photographic processing.
Filmstrips	Rolls of film easier to produce, ship, and store than individual slides. (Worth considering when large quantities of identical presentations are being produced. Can have high impact when coupled with recorded narration.	Special projectors required. (Hard to find.) Limited versatility. Order of visuals is fixed at photo facility.)
Movie	Shows motion. Suits any size audience. High interest level.	Projectors harder to come by and transport. Audience focuses on visual (rather than presenter). Darkened room eliminates note-taking and interaction during the presentation. High costs and long production time. Hard to revise.
Video Tape	Shows motion, high interest level. No photographic processing required. Easier and faster to produce than movies.	Larger audiences require multiple monitors. Audience focuses on visual (rather than presenter). Different recording formats require different playback equipment. (Tapes are not interchangeable.) Professional production costs are high.
Models, Mockups, and Props	Added "reality." High-impact value. Versatility. Props and products are readily available.	Models take time to prepare and can be costly. Use limited to smaller audience, depending on size of prop.

Sales Leadership

Southwest Region	41%
Northeast	23%
Middle Atlantic	17%
Central	12%
Pacific	7%

Sales Leadership

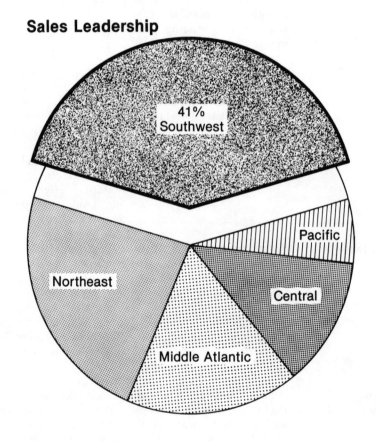

Pie charts (and other illustrations)
make relationships clearer and more interesting.

Maps

Maps show locations (offices, plants, markets, etc.) and how quantities are distributed geographically. They can also be used for size comparisons (How many times will Rhode Island fit into Alaska?), and as artistic backdrops, such as on title visuals. Next time you're tempted to merely list locations, try a map instead. Imagine what the information on the facing page would look like if a map were used showing the Middle Atlantic states at normal size and enlarging or reducing the other regions proportionately.

Block Diagrams, Schematics

These show how things flow, fit together, or relate to one another. The organization chart is a prime example. Using more than a dozen blocks on these charts is courting disaster. Fewer would be better. Consider showing just the major portions on an overall chart and then expanding on each portion with a piece of follow-up art.

Bar Charts

Bar charts come in a variety of styles. All are good for comparisons. In the simplest version, the bars extend horizontally and there is only one scale—the lengths of the bars. Sometimes there are two scales. Here the bars are usually arranged vertically with the height of the bars measuring quantity and the horizontal scale usually representing time.

More sophisticated bar charts can be prepared by dividing the bars into their component parts, increasing the number of comparisons that can be made. Also, sets of bars can be brought together for direct comparison of different categories (sales and assets, men and women, etc.). Other basic arrangements include the *sliding bar*, *deviation*, *range*, and *overlap* arrangements shown on page 61. Additional symbols can be added to any of these to show milestones, goals, current values, and the like.

Alpine Charts

In alpine charts the various values are connected to one another rather than to the base, forming a curve. Curves are much better than bar charts for showing trends—particularly where more than two items are involved. Curves are the most useful form of graphic presentation and far more are drawn than any other type. Most frequently the vertical scale represents dollars (or some other quantity) and the horizontal represents time. Many other combinations appear in engineering and other technical fields. Keep in mind that the length of the vertical axis in relation to the horizontal axis will have a marked effect on the impression given, as shown in the diagrams on page 62.

Since you should be using all your visuals in a horizontal format (more about that later), you needn't worry about the top curve. But suppose the format shown on the bottom produces a chart that is as flat as the plains of Kansas, and the minute variations are important. In this case, consider the "broken frame" or "depressed zero" curve. The illustration on page 63 shows what can be done. This technique accentuates the *differences* between totals. At the same time it can be deceiving in terms of the totals themselves. Make sure the scale is clearly marked and the break is shown.

The broken frame makes some technical people nervous, but there is another scale they love—the logarithmic (or log) scale. On the logarithmic scale, equal distances represent equal ratios. (See the illustrations on page 64.) Thus, the log scale can do things an arithmetic scale cannot. Often referred to as ratio charts, the log scales show the relative importance of change at various levels and the relative rate of change. For example, a one-dollar increase in the price of a one-dollar product is one-hundred percent, while the same increase on a five-dollar product would be only twenty percent. Yet an arithmetic scale would show both the same way.

A log scale would reflect the smaller percentage of growth. Thus these charts have a special usefulness for showing relative changes. For example, an arithmetic scale might show production rising by increasing amounts, whereas the log scale would present a more accurate picture, showing that production has been rising—but by *decreasing* percentages.

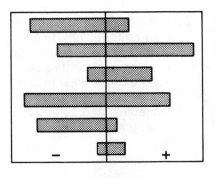

Sliding bar shows ratio of "pluses to minuses." (For example exports versus imports, proposals lost versus won.) The vertical line provides a base. Right means favorable, left unfavorable.

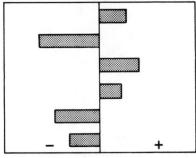

Deviation technique is similar. Vertical baseline divides pluses versus minuses in either/or situations. (For example, profit versus loss.)

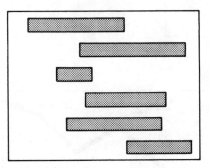

This variation shows **range,** as in the amount of time set aside for various phases in a schedule, or high-low stock values.

"Overlap" technique can show last year versus this year, goals versus performance, or how your organization stacks up against an industry average.

Types of bar charts

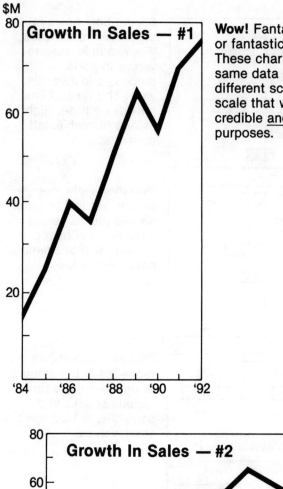

Wow! Fantastic growth or fantastic charting? These charts present the same data plotted on different scales. Pick a scale that will be credible <u>and</u> suit your purposes.

Effect of changing scale on impression

The broken frame or depressed zero curve will accentuate peaks and valleys, but you must indicate the break. Beware of the risk of misinterpretation.

Full-range scale vs. broken frame curve

The arithmetic version shows steady growth with a calamitous dip at the end. The logarithmic shows a decreasing <u>rate</u> of growth and puts the final dip in perspective. The first dip of only two units represents a twenty percent drop, whereas the final dip of fifteen units is also twenty percent.

Arithmetic and logarithmic plots

Color Versus Black-and-White

As proof of the desirability of color visuals over black-and-white, one need only consider the sales figures for television sets in this country. All those people aren't spending all that extra money purely as a status symbol. Color makes watching TV more interesting, more enjoyable. And, in a presentation, color can do even more. Color can be used to trace the flow or to code various parts, thus clarifying the message. It can even reinforce your message by using a simple underline or by using red for a "no," "stop," or "problem" message, and by using green for "go," "money," or "solution."

Unless you simply want to, there's no need to settle for black and white. Color pens can be used to add color to overhead transparencies, and the sensitized sheets used to make the transparencies come in a variety of colors. Even black-and-white photos can have a light blue, yellow, or sepia tint added to give them some semblance of color, and some added interest to your audience.

Do watch out for the rainbow or Joseph's cloak appearance—limit yourself to a few colors and then use them consistently.

Cartoons

Although they take a fair amount of skill to prepare, cartoons can add a little levity to a presentation, and are welcome in the proper circumstances. By definition, a cartoon shows things in an exaggerated way—the more exaggerated, the better.

Photographs can often be used as "cartoons" by adding a funny caption. For example, you might take a picture of a fortune teller and label it, "long-range planning." Or, gather up all the old brushes in your house, set them afire, shoot the scene, and label it, "Reduce brush fires." Many times a "bad" photo that would be thrown away has just the right facial expressions. Photos of children are particularly easy. Gather up all the pictures you can find and have a go at it. You should come up with a few good ones.

Sometimes a word chart alone can do the trick. A little while ago I had to give a presentation to some financial managers to justify my new departmental budget. Knowing that controllers are always on the lookout for extravagance, my first chart was a childish scrawl stating, "This presentation didn't cost much." They loved it.

Three-Dimensional Art

Unless one suffers from a vision problem, one sees things in three dimensions, giving one depth perception. Three-dimensional artwork can add another type of perception (understanding). For example, a three-dimensional cutaway is vastly superior to a two-dimensional cross-section in terms of realism and interest value. The extra preparation time is usually well worth the effort.

Photography

Photography automatically provides a three-dimensional atmosphere, a view of reality. Many times I have seen slide presentations in which the speaker had a professional artist draw some common object such as a mousetrap. Why pay an artist dollars to draw a mousetrap when you can buy one at the hardware store for a few pennies and then photograph it for a few pennies more? Even if an object costs more than a few pennies, it certainly costs far less than hiring a professional artist who would charge for a good drawing. Furthermore, the photographic treatment will be far more realistic—particularly with some shadows obtained by adding side lighting and standing the object on its end or elevating it from the surface with a hidden support.

Slides do require photographic processing, and you may elect not to use photography where artwork would be quicker and cheaper—especially if you are using charts where large photographic blowups would be required.

VISUAL TECHNIQUES

Now that the various types and styles are familiar to you, take a look at some visual techniques that will make your presentations more dynamic.

Dynamic Visuals

The term "dynamic" applied to a visual may mean that it is forceful, or that it actually moves, or both.

A touch of imagination can make a visual more forceful. Suppose you wanted to cite one of the basic truths your service function is based on, but you didn't want to look like you thought you had just discovered it. You could prepare a visual that looked like the old-fashioned stitchery on the Whitman Sampler candy box. The letters spelling out your point would appear as cross-stitching. Actual thread or yarn would be nice (if you have the time and the skill), but X's drawn in a cross-pattern with felt-tip color pens will also do the trick.

Certainly parts of a chart can be made to slide, "grow," or rotate, as can parts of overhead transparencies. There is even a polarizing technique that can be used to simulate motion on overheads and 35mm slides. Multiple-projector slide shows can also add a degree of animation. Keep in mind, however, that the motion should be used to make a point—not just for its gimmick value.

Progressive Disclosure

In themselves, "verbal visuals" or word charts, lists, and tables are perhaps the least dynamic type of aid. And yet, there is a technique that will greatly enhance their effectiveness. It's called progressive disclosure.

One of the problems with showing an audience a list of five or six items is that they may have reached item six while you are still talking about item three or four. Since your audience can think much faster than you can talk, this is only natural. But it doesn't make for a good presentation.

Of course, you can read all six items and then go back to explain them one by one. But this still supplies your listeners with an excuse to take a mental excursion. The cure is progressive disclosure—showing your audience each item at the rate you want them to consider it.

In the write-it-as-you-go presentation on a chalkboard, viewgraph, or chart, progressive disclosure simply "happens" as you move along. But this can be time consuming, and there are other techniques.

Using an overhead projector you can place a sheet of paper over the transparency, blocking out the light. Then slide the sheet down a step at a time, revealing as much as you choose. On charts, the same effect can be achieved by lightly taping a strip of blank paper over each line of text and pulling them off as you progress. Slides offer similar possibilities requiring only one piece of artwork. A six-step list would be shot in its entirety and six negative slides (white letters on black background) produced. Only the sixth slide would be used as is. Working "backwards," the sixth (final) line on the fifth slide would be opaqued or blanked out, then the fifth *and* sixth lines on the fourth slide, and so on. When shown in the reverse order, a normal progression or build-up will occur. A variation, called build-and-subdue, calls for toning down previous lines with a shade of gray, further highlighting the one currently under discussion.

Progressive disclosure is applicable to more than lists and tables. A complex series of overlying curves could be developed one curve at a time; areas of a plant can be shown with pieces of equipment to be moved or modified; side-by-side comparisons of new versus old can be made; or what's inside a piece of equipment can be displayed by removing the cover. The possibilities are endless.

Overhead transparencies can be used very effectively for this purpose. The material to be added is simply placed on another transparency that will be placed over the first at the proper moment. To ensure proper alignment, one side of the addition is usually taped to the base visual using pieces of transparent tape as hinges. Used in reverse, this same procedure can be used to take apart the composite image.

Similar effects can be obtained with flip charts, particularly in showing "old versus new," "ours versus theirs," or other side-by-side comparisons. In this case a piece of blank chart paper is cut vertically and placed over the right half of the table, drawing, or whatever so it obscures the new, improved version. At the proper time it is flipped back and—voila.

The pulloffs mentioned earlier have other uses. For example, picture a big dollar bill that peels away in various sized pieces to reveal a caption stating where that particular portion of income went. (This is an interesting variation of the pie chart approach.)

In addition to pulloffs for your charts, consider stick-ons. Suppose you had a list of alternatives and wanted to dismiss each one as you finished discussing it by sticking a "NO" on top, leading to a final "YES." (To avoid looking too authoritarian, you could ask the group's opinion on each item after you've finished making your point. Just in case, you might have a few "MAYBE's" standing by and, possibly, an extra "YES.") The same possibilities occur with arrows, stars, checkmarks, x-outs, O.K.'s, etc.

There are commercially available stick-ons in pads. 3M produces the Post-It™ pad in high visibility yellow in three sizes ranging from 1½ by 2 inches to 3 by 5 inches. These stick-ons can be moved about (reused) to show transfer of information in a computer, rearrangement of seating, etc. On a viewgraph, the same effect can be achieved with a small scrap of colored transparency, pushing it about as need be.

MULTI-IMAGE PRESENTATIONS

Most presentations involve a single projector with a single screen. However, the situation occasionally calls for something a little more sophisticated. Enter the multiple projector show. These shows can get as complicated and costly as you like (and can afford) with any number of projectors programmed by punched paper tapes or a computer. This section covers the simplest form, the sort of thing you can do for yourself.

Sometimes these are referred to as dual-screen presentations, but this is a misnomer, since an attempt should be made to use a single, large-width screen so there is no line (or screen edge) between images. Therefore, "dual-projector" would be more appropriate; however, the term generally used in the trade is "multi-image." Regardless of the name, the important thing is how to improve your presentations using these techniques.

Although you can certainly get more information on a wide screen by using two projectors and still have it be readable, that is *not* the purpose of a multi-image presentation. Rather than adding more *detail*, the purpose is to add more *interest*. This is usually done by having a photo slide next to one with text or a curve. A movie can also be run next to a slide. (Don't forget to insert a black blank to make sure that side of the screen goes dark while the movie is being shown.)

The first time I ever saw a two-projector presentation, the technique was used very effectively for describing a number of components that made up a piece of equipment. As a photo of each component was shown on the left side, a series of slides on the right presented first its nomenclature and location, then its electrical characteristics, then its mechanical characteristics, then its performance curve, and so on. Then a photo of the next component accompanied by its nomenclature and location was presented and the process was repeated. Thus, the audience was never in doubt as to which particular component was under discussion at any given time, and the illustration slide added interest and a point of reference.

Note that the illustration slide was "held" on the left without being repeated as the series on the right progressed. There is no need to insert duplicate slides so that both sides change simultaneously with each sequence. In fact, repeating slides for this purpose will only tend to distract the audience.

Normally, in presentations of this type, the speaker works with a projectionist to avoid having to worry about whether to push the right or left button. The speaker cues the projectionist, who pushes the correct button by referring to a cue sheet. (See the sample cue sheet below.)

Another valuable advantage of a dual projector setup is its usefulness in making "before and after" comparisons. This is usually done as a side-by-side progression: that is, showing "before" on the left next to a black blank slide, then adding "after" on the right.

One of the problems that can arise in a dual-projector presentation is a hideous color combination between the left and right slides. I've seen some that would drive an audience to nausea, given enough time. This is usually the result of the speaker pulling slides at random from his or her desk drawers and then attempting to put together a dual-image presentation. Certainly some existing slides will be used, but the presentation should be planned for side-by-side viewing using storyboards similar to the one shown on page 71. Once the order is established, every effort should be made to stick with it to avoid mismatched colors.

Another good technique is to use a black background for text slides with white or yellow words—or both in combination, yellow for the title and white for the body. The black background avoids

Talk Title **Manufacturing Improvements**

Adv		Right Title/Description	Tray Pos	Left Title/Description	Tray Pos
L	R	Title	1	Speaker's Photo	1
L	R	Aerial View	2	Acreage statistics	2
L	R	List of Departments	3	Blank	3
	R	↓ ↓	–	Employee #'s	4
	R	↓ ↓	–	Hourly Rates	5
	R	↓ ↓	–	Defects Ratios	6
L	R	~~~~	~~~~	~~~~	~~~~
	R	New Equipment	13	Capital Investments	16
L	R	Robotic Welder	14	✦Movie✦(Blank)	17
L		Cost Figures	15	↓	–
	R	↓ ↓	–	5-Year Saving Curve	18
L	R	Automated Wire-Wrap	16	Photo	19

Projectionist's cue sheet for multi-image presentation

any color mismatch with the slide on the other side. It will also prevent a bright word slide from overpowering a color illustration slide. Finally, since the black background will result in a slide that has no projected "edge," it eliminates overlapping images or gaps at the center of the screen, or having one slide misaligned in height.

Although alignment can be a problem, you shouldn't rule out using both projectors to project a "single" image from one side of the screen to the other. This can be very effective if you want to show something really big, such as a mountain range, sea surface, city, long lists, rows of products, etc., where the subject matter lends itself to this technique.

Try to put titles on one side. If they must run across both sides, never make the split in the middle of a word. Whatever the subject, care should be taken in shooting and mounting the slides and aligning the projectors. Then the audience will be able to adjust to any minor misalignments.

Another good use of dual images can be found in humorous warm-up presentations for sales meetings, retirements, banquets, and the like. Here a photo is usually presented on the left, next to a black blank. After a short period to let the image sink in, a funny caption (in small but readable type) is flashed next to the photo. When the laughter reaches its peak, both sides go blank for a

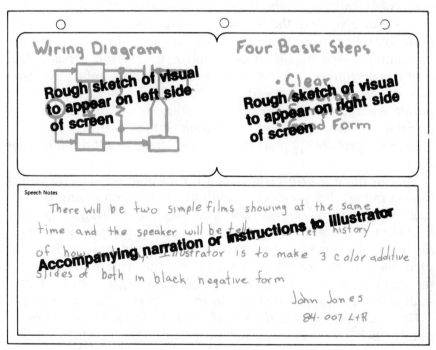

Storyboard form for dual projector presentation

moment and then the process repeats itself. If the photo is so hilarious that it becomes the punch line, a "straight" caption can be used first.

This technique can be accompanied by a live narration. However, my own preference is to use some fast-moving music to avoid having the words on the screen compete with the narration. The technique requires a special knack for this sort of thing, inside knowledge of the subject, and the ability to come up with a hundred ideas and then use only ten. And you usually need a fairly large audience to get the necessary reaction.

Multiple-projector shows require more planning, plus larger screens and more projectors to carry (or rent), but they are really not that difficult and they certainly increase the interest level. Consider multi-image presentations where you need impact and where the presentation is important enough or will be given frequently enough to justify the extra effort.

REVIEWING THE ROUGH VISUALS

The time to edit your visuals is now, when they are in the rough sketch or storyboard form, not after all the time and money has been spent finishing them. Here are some things to look for:

Are your visuals in the horizontal format? Audiences prefer the horizontal to the vertical. (And so do projectionists, since the horizontal image makes more effective use of the screen.) Our vision is peripheral, and our eyes can cover a horizontal area faster and more easily. The vertical format tempts us to make seven points whereas we would be more likely to use only five in the horizontal. Also, the lower the bottom of the chart or screen, the greater the probability people in the back rows won't be able to see it.

Do you have a title visual? You didn't plan on starting with a log-log curve, did you? Your audience needs something to help them stop "excursioning," and you need something to get you through the introductory, "Good afternoon ladies and gentlemen, my topic for today is . . ." Your title visual should include the topic, identified in six words or *less*; your name (particularly if the pronunciation or spelling is unusual); your organization's name, seal, or logo; the specific date; and some "interest" art, if possible.

How about the rest of the titles? Do they summarize or make the point? "Schedule" doesn't make a point. "Delivery in 3 Weeks" does! Try to get a sales message in your titles. "Next Year's Preakness Winner" is going to get a lot more attention than "Horse, Side

View." Rhetorical questions are another interest grabber—for example, "What has been learned?" And, of course, there's always "Benefits."

Too many verbal visuals? Word charts should be limited in terms of the number used and the number of words on any given chart. Remember, pictures lighten visuals, words make them heavier. Use bullets (•), sock dots (●), "interest" art, color, and progressive disclosure to help break the monotony. More than three word charts in a row without any visual break is dangerous. After the third such chart they all look the same.

As to the number of words on a single visual, try for a title plus a *maximum* of six lines with a *maximum* of six words in each line. For tables, try to stay within five lines deep and four columns across.

Will it be readable? There is a group of speakers who tell their audiences, "I know you can't read this in the back row, but . . ." I hope their reward for irritating audiences in this manner is to spend eternity engraving the Lord's Prayer on the head of a pin.

Often the cause of unreadable visuals, particularly slides and viewgraphs, traces to their being shot directly from printed material. After all, if you can read it on an 8½-by-11-inch page, you ought to be able to read the same material on a six-foot-wide screen. The truth is that viewers in the last row may be as much as seventy feet away, and to them that screen will only be two inches wide. So while the projector may magnify, the end result for some of the audience may be reduction. The art for visuals and that for printed matter require distinctly different approaches. Visuals require less detail, fewer words, larger letters, simpler grids, and heavier lines. Recycling or at least reprocessing will be required. The KISS formula (Keep It Short and Simple) was never more important.

Does each visual achieve unity? That is, does it develop one, and only one main point? Or, is it full of points competing for the audience's attention? Even in technical presentations an audience should be able to comprehend your visual in less than fifteen seconds, and your accompanying narration should keep it up there *no longer than one minute.* (Ideally, the narration will add detail and emphasis, not explain the visual.) Two of the major causes of poor presentations are:

- Too few visuals
- Too much detail on a single visual

Each of these shortcomings feeds on the other.

Now let's move on to our next to last topic.

MAKING YOUR VISUALS

If you are part of a large organization that includes an art department, getting your visuals produced is quite simple. All they will want is a reasonable amount of time and a charge number. Similar professional services, which are available to the public, have phototypesetters and other equipment that can make lettering a snap. Depending on how much value you put on your own time, their charges are often a bargain. But you don't always have the time or a budget, and in some cases, you don't want to look too "fancy." In that case you can easily do your own low-cost visuals.

Low cost does not mean poor quality or unprofessional results. These shortcomings are usually the result of lack of time and effort *and* not knowing a few tricks of the trade.

Use the right supplies. You can find some of the things you will need in your company storeroom, or in an office supplies or art supplies store. Such things as transfer lettering, pressure sensitive tapes and patterns, transparency pens, chart markers, clip-book art, and stock or made-to-order slides are available. One way to find out what's available is to ask. Another is to browse through the stores or catalogs. Organizations you might want to contact are listed in the resources section at the back of this book.

Use the KILL formula. Much like its partner, KISS (Keep It Short and Simple), the KILL formula means Keep It Large and Legible. In order for your charts to be readable from fifty feet away, the letter size will have to be *at least* two inches high, with the same amount of space between the lines.

If you're using color, you need contrast—dark letters on light backgrounds. (Vice versa is nice on slides.)

If you're using slides, it may be a little hard to determine adequate letter size. There are two ways to go about it. The first is to use the 6W test, wherein you move away to a distance six times the width of the visual and then take a look. (This also applies to viewgraphs.) The other is to hold the finished slide up to the light and attempt to read it with your naked eye. If the visual fails either test, you should try again.

Cut, cut, cut. Eliminate any unnecessary lines, symbols, or words. Don't use "in the event that", use "if." Imagine that you're doing a roadside billboard. Simplify as much as possible. Deletion automatically places more emphasis on what's left. On the other hand, spell out any abbreviations or acronyms that *might* be confusing.

Be creative. Add interest art. If you're talking about time, add a clock. Words like heat, cold, misalignment, vibration, growth, and drift all suggest an imaginative lettering style. If you're talking about going from dollars to cents, you might start with a chart showing a large dollar sign. Then, as you talk, you progressively peel away parts of it until what you have remaining is a cents sign. The only limit in this area is your own imagination.

Show the customer's system. Let's suppose you make disc brakes and that's what your presentation is about, keeping in mind that your customer makes buses or airplanes in which your brakes are eventually installed. Wherever possible, you will want to show or relate to the total system. Your title visual provides a good opportunity for this and gets your presentation off to a good start. Later it may be appropriate to show where your equipment is located in the total system or how it attaches. You'll also want to show their system at the end of your talk by mentioning benefits, conclusions, and recommendations.

The nuts'n'bolts of flip charts. Leave at least two inches of free space all the way around. This is particularly important at the top (so that the gripper bar won't cover part of your title) and at the bottom (where there may be some curling from having been rolled up). If the chart paper is thin, use double sheets (taped or stapled together) to prevent showthrough or premature disclosure of the next chart, and to prevent bleedthrough of the markers. Make corrections by mortising—that is, put a clean sheet directly beneath the area to be changed and cut through both with a razor blade. You will now have a clean piece of paper that will *exactly* fit the hole in the original. A little tape on the back and no one will ever know.

Flip chart pads measuring 27 by 34 inches are available for under ten dollars. In a pinch, manila file folders can be opened out to make suitable charts for small audiences. (Needless to say, they are easily filed when you're finished.)

Doing your own overheads. The most glaring mistake you see in this area is the use of office typewriters to prepare the visuals. Even the large typefaces for the interchangeable-element typewriters are marginal at best. If you don't have transfer or photo-composed lettering at your disposal, try hand lettering. Pens are available that are specifically designed for working on transparencies. A one-quarter-inch ruled sheet below the acetate will ensure alignment and neatness.

By all means, use frames on your viewgraphs. They will:

- Keep the transparencies from sticking together.
- Give you a place to write "stage whispers."
- Block spillover light from the projector.

- Provide a firm base on which to tape overlays for progressive disclosures.

A service for turning 35mm color slides into overhead transparencies is available through 3M's service centers. Most office copy shops can also make a transparency from your black-and-white original.

Producing 35mm slides. Here are a few things to keep in mind if you are shooting your own slides. First, clean up the area. Next, add people for interest and scale. Now get in closer. If you are showing a person doing something, the hands and what is being worked on are probably more important than the rest. (If you are working from an existing photo, crop it and reshoot.) Sometimes photographs can be shot directly from printed matter without the halftone dot pattern becoming too obvious.

Artwork for slides should be prepared in the 2:3 ratio of the finished slide. (For example, six inches high by nine inches wide.) Simple word slides can be prepared using a carbon ribbon typewriter and a three-inch-high by four-and-one-half-inch-wide typing area. (Shoot it as a negative and consider using pastel dyes or overlays to add color.) Of course, transfer or photo-composed lettering will usually work best. Three-dimensional letters can also be used.

Personal computers can be used with any of several hard-copy devices to make good do-it-yourself visuals. Recently, some major companies have been offering professional-level computer-produced slides. Xerox, 3M, and Genigraphics® have systems on the market that really bring the computer age to slide production. Buying your own equipment will cost $450,000 for a complete system, or $17,000 for a personal computer and modem link. But the service is available from company outlets at prices approaching $40 per slide. Among the advantages are:

- Speed (overnight, or in an hour with your own system)
- Retrieval (stored on floppy disk)
- Easy revisions
- Up to 4,096 colors
- Various type fonts and sizes
- Automatic conversion from spread sheet (tabular) form to pie charts, bar charts, graphs, etc.

Three-dimensional models. With a little skill (and some work) you can turn out credible models using styrofoam and other materials at hand. If the "equipment" is in existence and almost square or rectangular, you can make a 3-D model by carefully photographing all four sides, mounting the enlarged photos on cardboard or foamcore, cutting along the outline, and gluing the pieces together. Engineering or architectural drawings will yield similar results.

In their book, *In Search of Excellence—Lessons From America's Best-Run Companies*, Thomas Peters and Robert Waterman tell of a balsa wood model (constructed out of materials purchased for fifteen dollars at a local hobby shop and assembled over a weekend in a hotel room) that helped a team of engineers from Boeing win the contract for the U.S. Air Force B-52 bomber.[10]

THAT'S ALL, FOLKS

Of course, that isn't all. When I was planning and organizing this book, I stored all my notes for each chapter in the largest envelopes I could find. This chapter overflowed its envelope, and I still haven't covered everything. One could easily write an entire book on visuals, and some people have. Two such books are *How to Put on Dynamic Meetings* by Chester K. Guth and Stanley S. Shaw, and *Planning and Producing Audiovisual Materials* by Jerrold E. Kemp. But perhaps the best way to learn about how to use visuals is the "hard" way—by doing it. You'll find a few more tips in Chapter 7, Practice Makes Perfect.

CHAPTER SIX

Selling Yourself and Your Ideas

ALL OF US ARE PART-TIME SALESPEOPLE

WHILE I PLANNED this chapter I thought, "What are you doing writing this? You're no salesman."

But that's not true. While we may not be selling a product, all of us are selling ourselves and our ideas every day. This is particularly true in presentations.

Throughout this chapter, the terms "sell" and "customer" are used. These broad terms can denote anyone (our managers, spouses, co-workers or others) we are trying to persuade to buy either our products or ideas.

In giving presentations, many speakers approach their task as merely to inform their audience, and the results are usually lackluster. The better speakers present ideas *and* also persuade and promote—they sell.

To some, selling is a dirty word. Those who would demean selling think in terms of the door-to-door huckster, ignoring the fact that *Vice-President, Sales* adorns some of the finest desks and doors in the United States. Or, they feel that successful salespeople are born—just like speakers, no doubt—when both selling and speaking are learnable skills.

There are other reasons for avoiding selling, but perhaps the biggest is fear of rejection—indeed, most of the other reasons may be subliminal cop-outs for this particular one. Fear of rejection traces back to the earliest moments of our childhood and stays with us all our days. Successful salespeople overcome this barrier by learning not to take personally the rejection of a product or idea. Better still, they figure out what to do differently after they experience a loss, and press on to the next opportunity. They have a commitment that takes them beyond the fear of risk. And, above all, they employ strategies they know will maximize their chances of winning. We will be taking a look at some of these sales strategies later in this chapter. But first, let's establish their tie to presentations.

THE WAY YOU PRESENT INDICATES HOW WELL YOU WILL PRODUCE

Audiences form an immediate impression of your ability to perform by how well you come across in your presentations. Thus, your presentations are a reflection of your total professional capability. Being right just isn't enough, you must also be persuasive. To do this, you must first be sure of yourself and then radiate positive emotional stimuli throughout your presentation.

In fact, your presentation begins before you have even opened your mouth. It begins the moment you walk through the door or toward the lectern. Make sure you are well-groomed. Smile. If any hands are offered, grasp them firmly. Let the audience know you are in control—both of yourself and the situation.

Be Positive—Sell Weddings, Not Funerals

Dr. Norman Vincent Peale and his book *The Power of Positive Thinking* have provided inspiration to a host of sales personnel and others. One of my favorite stories in this area comes from Russ Johnston, a salesman, who says:

> You've got to have the right perspective to succeed in selling. When Goliath came against the Israelites, the soldiers all thought, "Wow! He's so big we can never kill him!" David looked at him and said, "He's so big I can't miss."[11]

Elsewhere in this book the evils of canned presentations were discussed. But good presentations do, indeed, come in cans: "I can," "You can," "We can."

Given the right circumstances, you can transfer your own positive outlook to the audience and get them to give you a positive reaction. Make sure your audience knows where you are coming from and what your recommendations are. If you appear unconvinced, wishy-washy, or uncommitted, they will be very unlikely to give you a go-ahead. Avoid hedging. Instead of saying, "I think," use "I'm sure" wherever possible. Don't talk about how hard it was to develop your new technique, talk about how well it works. And, don't read your talk!

Abraham Lincoln once said, "If you would win a man to your cause, first convince him that you are his sincere friend." So, you want to be friendly, credible, somewhat informal, sincere, and authoritative (and—perhaps—thrifty, brave, clean, and reverent, too). Reading your talk can prevent any or all of these traits.

Improving Your Personal Sales Ability

Often, a competition can be so close that the customer picks the presenter as much as the product. In his book *The New Oratory*, Anthony Jay says:

> I keep hearing about decisions made after totally unemotional logical discussion based exclusively on objective facts, but only in management books. Most narrow decisions, I am convinced, come down more often than anyone yet accepts to primitive tribal acclamation, to a man or a small group of men winning the confidence and respect of another group. I do not even think it wrong that it should be so—very often this is in fact the most important remaining consideration. But we are taking a great risk if we are not aware of it when we are casting our presentations. I doubt if an unsuitable group can effectively persuade their audience that they are suitable, but I have no doubt at all that a suitable one can in the course of a presentation convince them that they are unsuitable.[12]

Part of what Jay is saying is that to be most effective, one should try to match the presenter(s) to the audience, picking individuals who already know the customers and are compatible. Failing this, one would seek out presenters who are at least credible, likeable, capable, and self-assured. But what if you are it, for better or worse?

Well, there are ways to shade things toward the better. One way is to develop that elusive quality known as charisma, and one way to build charisma is to do something new:

- Find a *new* hobby.
- Join a *new* group.
- Read a *new* type of book.
- Visit a *new* town.
- Try a *new* food or drink.

Any of these can help ease burn-out or the blahs and make you a more interesting, more persuasive personality. One word of caution, however: it's not just how interesting *you* are, but how interested you are in the *other person* that will help you sell.

Now the stage is set for persuasion.

THE PROCESS OF PERSUASION

Look up the word persuade in a thesaurus and you will find many synonyms: influence, win over, coax, convince, make willing, induce, convert, sell, and so forth. Behind these words lies a process that is rooted as much in emotion as in logic. Anthony Jay talks of an "intellectual judo . . . using the force of the other man's opinions and prejudices to win your argument," and he cautions against wrestling when you should use that judo. "You have to get inside his mind at the planning stage and build your presentation on the foundation of his knowledge, prejudices, attitudes, experience, and needs."[13] These needs can be for a product, for economic benefits, or even for psychic gratification (for example, the customer's desired self-image can create a psychic need). The customer's experience will include not only past successes and failures, but habits and even moral upbringing. Prejudices include all the obvious ones plus smoking, eating, and drinking habits. Find out what "bugs" your customer/manager. Modern television commercials to the contrary, there is absolutely no way you can antagonize and persuade at the same time in a presentation.

Good salespeople not only know their subjects well, they also know their customers. They do this not in an attempt to be manipulative, but out of honest concern for their customers' needs.

ASSESSING CUSTOMER NEEDS

If you've ever taken a course called Marketing 101, you may remember that selling consists of identifying customers' needs and then influencing the customers to work with you to satisfy those needs.

The process starts with gathering all the information you can on the customers' business: Volume. Market Share. Their Competition. Profit. Problems. Requirements. Expectations. This advance work will allow you to talk to the customers in their own language, not so you can tell them their business (they already know it and will resent such attempts as being arrogance on your part), but so you will be able to ask educated questions that will give them a chance to tell you more that you need to know. Other items you will want to consider include: your competition, availability of funds, who the real decisionmakers are, and past track records.

Now focus on their specific needs. To be a seller, you must have a product or an idea that will do more for your customers than the money or other resources in their possession. Unsatisfied needs are prime motivators. Determine the need. Ask yourself whether the customers will relate personally to your solution. Will it appeal to their special interests to be stylish, avoid trouble, and save time or money? Next, design your presentation to these interests and you will significantly improve your chances for acceptance.

In their book *In Search of Excellence—Lessons from America's Best-Run Companies,* Thomas Peters and Robert Waterman cite an outstanding example of how knowing your customer can lead to a successful sale:

> Another friend described for us why, in a recent major computer system purchase for a hospital, he chose International Business Machines. "Many of the others were ahead of IBM in technological wizardry," he noted. "And heaven knows their software is easier to use. But IBM alone took the trouble to get to know us. They interviewed extensively up and down the line. They talked our language, no mumbo jumbo on computer innards. Their price was fully twenty-five percent higher. But they provided unparalleled guarantees of reliability and service. They even went so far as to arrange a back-up connection with a local steel company in case our system crashed. Their presentations were to the point. Everything about them smacked of assurance and success. Our decision, even with severe budget pressure, was really easy."[14]

LOVE THY CUSTOMERS

A couple is talking. Suddenly one asks, "Do you love me?" And the answer is, "Of course!" To which the first replies, "You never show it!" Obviously, you "love" your customers. And you had better show it! One way is to acknowledge their importance.

Napoleon once said, "Ask me for anything—except time." Today he might say, "Time is money." Time (and attention spans) become more and more critical as you go up the management/customer ladder. An executive's time is extremely valuable and could easily be filled with things other than listening to your presentation. In seeking an audience, prepare a one-page interest grabber and then present this proposition in person or over the phone. If possible, ask for only ten minutes. (You can say a lot in ten minutes. Just look at the thirty- and sixty-second TV spots.) Be sure to state that's all *you* need. Then suggest the listeners leave some time open in case *they* would be interested in further discussion.

Once you have your appointment, be punctual. Build in extra time to guarantee on-time arrival. You may run into construction, heavy traffic, transportation breakdowns, an accident, or other delays. Don't rush; plan on killing some time in the parking lot or in the reception area. Remember that in some big industrial complexes, it may take fifteen minutes to get someone to meet you and escort you to the individual's office.

If you are running late, be sure to call and explain the difficulty and ask *permission* to come ahead anyway.

If you control the meeting room setup, you can make the audience feel important by providing attractive place settings (name tags, note pads, water, and agendas). Note pads can even be "personalized" to a specific meeting. Agendas can be prepared as small booklets containing a schedule, a list of key personnel and their telephone numbers, and a local map.

By all means you will want to remember those all-important words "please" and "thank you," but even more so, you will want to remember the customers' names. Dale Carnegie says the two most important words in the English language are YOUR NAME. And, if it's true with you, it's certainly true with your customers.

With a little advance preparation, you can make your customers feel like old friends (see page 15). Even without it, you can still do a credible job. When introduced, make sure you get the name. If you don't, ask that it be repeated. Find a way to use it in the conversation as soon as possible, and associate the name with the individual by matching the two in some way if at all possible. Take on large groups one at a time and don't be embarrassed to check back on names you think you've "gotten."

SALES STRATEGIES

Where do you go from, "Nice weather we've been having," or, "Did you have a good trip?" This is the critical juncture where you must capture the customers' interest. You must shift their attitudes from a skeptical "So what have you got?" to "Oh boy! How can I get one?" as you present your ideas. Ideas, fortunately, are like eggs— they can be served in many ways. You might elect to open with:

- A startling statement or question. ("Do you know that one of your departments is literally throwing away $70,000 each year?")
- Major benefits. ("Rearranging our outpatient center would save time and money, and improve the quality of service.")
- Product demonstrations, models, or mockups. (Here you actually show that something is smaller, works better, or is easier to handle—perhaps in a side-by-side, old-versus-new demonstration.)
- A statement of customer needs (e.g., setting up a "problem/solution" approach).

Notice that in each of these approaches you put your advantages up front by telling the customers why they should listen and, thus, winning their interest.

Sledgehammer or Velvet Hammer?

You can knock something down with a sledgehammer or stroke it with a velvet hammer. If you are demolishing a building you would use the former. Trying to get a cat to purr would call for the latter. The approach for people lies somewhere in between.

There's an excellent example of salesmanship in Meredith Willson's musical *The Music Man*. A supersalesman, Professor Harold Hill, comes to River City, Iowa, selling band instruments. None of the other salesmen can understand why Hill does so well. "Why, he doesn't even know the territory." He soon shows them why in the song "Ya Got Trouble," pointing out that it's "Trouble with a capital T, and that rhymes with P and P stands for Pool," informing anyone who will listen that the new pool table installed at the billiard parlor will soon be the downfall of the town. From there it's a short jump to the solution—a boy's band—and the upbeat, foot-stomping song, "Seventy-six Trombones."

There's a great marketing lesson there, and it's worth heeding. What if Professor Harold Hill had started with "Seventy-six Trombones" and either dropped "Ya Got Trouble," or saved it for last? Would he have been as effective? Of course not. "No Sir-ree!"

The technique Harold Hill used is sometimes called "setting up a straw man" (need or problem) which you can then knock away with your solution. This might even involve the fear of the competition doing something faster or more cheaply, or the fear of falling behind technologically.

Both of these techniques can be used effectively if used with caution. Be sure you know when enough is enough. Don't overwhelm your customers. Sometimes they will want to push the answer around until it becomes *their* answer. Let them! When this happens they "own" the solution.

"Reading" your audience by using good eye contact can tell you if you are in danger of overwhelming them. And encouraging their participation through questions and answers can lead the way toward "ownership."

The Soft-Sell Approach

With few exceptions, most of us are more comfortable with the soft-sell approach—particularly if we are on the receiving end. Let me quickly point out that "soft-sell" does not in any way indicate less effort or enthusiasm on your part. It's more of a perception on the part of the receiver.

None of us would grab a customer by the lapels and shout, "Now, look!" But there are other ways to overwhelm a customer. For example, are you taking a "committee" with you to make the presentation? When you and your group outnumber the customers, it puts them on the defensive or encourages them to call in their staffs, changing the nature of the meeting. You might want to take along one of your own brass or one expert, but any more will decrease the intimacy and/or make you seem less capable.

Instead of beating customers over the head with how great your product is, you might invite them to join you in constructing a "key factors chart" showing how your product compares with the competition's. Let them identify whether each factor gets a plus or minus in each column, and then discuss the logical choice.

Another aspect of the soft sell is to use phrases such as, "I'm here merely to point out something. Any decisions will be in your hands." And then make sure your tone of voice matches this statement throughout your presentation.

The poker player who holds a full house or better can, of course, afford to be soft-spoken. Let's suppose you have a multi-functional piece of equipment that does the work of three separate pieces currently in use, at a reduction in overall cost. Obviously, the user is not going to throw away the equipment now in service. But you have a very strong case for replacements or new installations. Make sure they fully understand the one-for-three benefit. Then, you can make them an offer they can't refuse (or at least can't ignore).

One more way to avoid overwhelming your audience is to start on familiar ground. Start with principles they already know or agree with. Then move on to the more complicated or opposite view. As the information becomes more complicated, cut down on the shake, rattle, and roll data. Give the audience only as much as they need to understand and to agree. In presenting opposing views, start "slowly." Remember Mark Antony's speech in Shakespeare's *Julius Caesar*? Because of the sensitive situation following Caesar's assassination, Mark Antony started, "Friends, Romans, countrymen . . . I come to bury Caesar, not to praise him." Indeed, by the time he finished he had praised Caesar quite a bit.

Certainly you won't start by telling your audience what it's going to cost them. (Unless the cost is so low you want to startle them.) Instead, start by telling them what your product or service will do for them. Thus, when cost does come up, you have set the stage for answering the question with, "Not as much as you might think."

Sometimes you can make the cost seem like less by showing how it might be shared by two or more parties, or how the equipment might perform more than one function. In the case of replacement, it's possible that the new approach will pay for itself over a period of time. For example, you can find the costs of repairing older, less reliable equipment, or the cost of the increased energy it uses, and deduct those costs from the new. Or, you can cite the basic investment in the existing equipment and the advantages of updating it with a relatively inexpensive modification (compared to replacement). In either case the customer is saving money in the long run.

Be Flexible, Give the Customer a Chance to Talk

Have you ever wondered why God gave us two ears and only one mouth? So we could enjoy stereo? Perhaps. But I wonder if He just might have been trying to tell us that we ought to do twice as much listening as talking.

In giving a presentation it's hard to spend *twice* as much time listening as talking. But, don't neglect this important sales strategy before, during, and after your presentation.

Don't launch into your presentation too quickly. Try to find out more about the customers. They may want to talk about their backgrounds, desires, interests, ambitions, or motives. This is particularly valuable at the onset of a less formal, one-on-one presentation or at the coffee session that may precede meeting with a larger group. Try to set up a process where they talk and you listen. Give them feedback, reinforcement, agreement. Focus on *them*.

During your talk, don't insist on plowing through your script, dismissing any customer comments as quickly as possible so that you can get on with it. If someone in the audience says, "That's an interesting idea, have you thought about trying it on . . .?", don't say, "Yes, we've already thought of that, now, as I was saying . . ." Given a chance, the customer may tell your story for you. The presentation *really* begins when the customer starts talking. Welcome the two-way flow and control it. If you ignore it, you will miss valuable clues, antagonize the customer, and probably lose the sale.

Instead, use effective questions to keep the dialogue going. A general rule in selling is that the person who asks the questions has control. You can ask questions to determine needs, discover likes and dislikes, check agreement or listening, feel out objections, determine whether the customer is ready to "buy" or whether you should keep selling, and other information. Questions such as, "Can you tell me more about that?" or, "What do you think?" will often flush out your quarry. After you ask, be patient. Let the customer answer fully.

If you've really "heard" your customers' needs, you may be able to make the sale by explaining a single aspect of your product or idea. Anyone can tell a customer one thing. The good listeners make it the *right* thing.

"You Can Rest Assured"

Naturally, the customer is looking for a definite commitment— assurances—on your part. These take the form of promises, which in order to have teeth are sometimes backed with penalties in terms of reduced price or increased quantities for nonperformance.

But there is another type of assurance that we touched on a few moments ago when we were discussing letting the customer do the talking for you, and that is the testimonial. Having a third party do your talking can make your listeners less skeptical, particularly if the third party is an independent authority on the subject.

Testimonials can be delivered in person (or even by satellite link), via movies or video tape, on audio tape accompanied by slides of the authority, *short* quotes on charts, or even copies of a letter. Be sure to ask permission to quote, and if the individual is present, introduce him or her properly.

IBM uses this technique quite effectively in selling computers to small businesses, giving potential customers a chance to see how businesses similar to theirs have profited by installing a computer.

Westinghouse and other companies have also used the same technique to allow customers to share their thoughts on quality with employees.

I once saw a testimonial save the job of a representative for a leading manufacturer of projection equipment. Problems arose in demonstrating a sound/slide system and the rep, who found himself unable to operate the equipment, began making excuses in front of forty potential buyers *and* his district sales manager. As the noose grew tighter, the rep was saved by a projectionist in the audience who came to his rescue with an unsolicited testimonial about how he had used the same type of equipment countless times and had never had the slightest problem.

The projectionist was somewhat unkempt in a flannel shirt with his T-shirt showing, and his beard, long hair, and mode of dress set him apart from the others in the room. But *everybody* listened! Unfortunately, the rep in his three-piece suit didn't. If he had, he probably would have been smart enough to ask the projectionist if he could fix the problem during a short coffee break.

Product Demos and Samples

No other type of sales presentation can equal the product demonstration. It allows you to show the actual product and why it is better than its fourteen competitors.

If your product is small enough to hold, hold it at chest level as you talk about its benefits. Then tell the audience what to look for as you put it to action. Let the way you handle the product show your esteem.

When demonstrating models or equipment, be sure to
hold the item high enough for the audience to see.

You may even have a chance to give the customers some hands-on experience using it, or possibly even leave behind a sample. Everyone likes something for nothing. If you're lucky, they will test it. Even if it just sits on their desks awhile, it will serve as a reminder. Be sure your telephone number is attached.

Selling by Semantics

Using the wrong words in a sales presentation can block the sale. And, while using the right ones may not clinch it, they certainly don't hurt.

As a comparison, consider:
- Cheap and flimsy *vs.* inexpensive and lightweight.
- Council for Responsible Nutrition *vs.* Vitamin Lobby.

Some words can be loaded in two directions, depending which side of the fence you are on:

consumer advocates	pro-choice
environmentalists	pro-life
fair trade	productivity
free enterprise	right-to-work laws

You also need increased sensitivity to words that might be considered sexist or even racist.

Try these words for positive impact:

assured	first	proven
bargain	free	quality
best	guarantee	reliable
biggest	heavy-duty	results
compact	improved	rugged
demonstrated	long-life	safety
discovery	money	save
easy	new	smallest
efficient	only	you

And be sure you back up any opinions with facts.

Startling statements or attention-getters ought to be prefaced as such:

- "I know you will find it hard to believe. We had to double-check our figures when we first ran across this, but . . ."

- "Now pay attention to these sales numbers, because they get pretty big. There are eleven districts with two systems per district—that's twenty-two systems—and each system has eighteen terminals, for a grand total of three-hundred-and-ninety-six terminals!"

Look for hard-hitting slogans or themes that tie your major benefits into a neat, compact package:

- "An aerodynamic solution to an aerodynamic problem."
- "Separation means stability."
- "Easy to operate. Drives like a car."

SOMETIMES YOU HAVE TO BE A DIPLOMAT, AS WELL AS A SALESPERSON

Sometimes it will seem as though you've been handed a gallon bucket and told to go milk a cobra. As mentioned earlier, when you have to persuade an audience that might be hostile, move slowly. Don't establish your position too early. If the audience is well-educated, you would be wise to present both sides. Sometimes a minus can even be turned into a plus. For example:

> Transporting the unit in the horizontal position will require that it be thoroughly sealed so that the hydraulic fluid won't leak out. However, sealing the unit in this manner will actually prove to be an advantage since it will ensure both cleanliness and lubrication during transit.

One must always stay alert to the possibility of changing negatives into positives. Once I was in a meeting where an engineer was explaining a trailer that was full of test equipment which was available to the electrical utility industry for use at various power plants. As he explained the pieces of test equipment and their functions, someone asked, "But haven't you been having a lot of problems with this equipment?" Indeed they had been, and the engineer quickly told them so, ticking off three examples on his fingers. But then he quickly shifted gears to point out that that was precisely the beauty of installing all the test equipment in the new trailer. It had eliminated the problems by providing a permanent yet mobile installation within a controlled environment.

On another occasion I was called in to do some consulting on a coal-fired electrical generating plant. The manufacturer was worried because the plant wasn't producing quite as much power as had been specified, resulting in reduced income for the utility and raising the possibility of litigation.

I had studied all the various documents and became more and more confused. During a meeting to discuss the problem, I found myself put on the spot for an opinion on how to approach the customer. Somewhat at a loss for words—and certainly at a loss for ideas—I decided to try the "ask *them* a question" technique. "So, what's the *good* news?" I asked. Silence. And then someone in the far reaches of the room slowly answered, "Well, for the amount of electricity it produces, it burns a lot less coal than we ever thought." Sensing an opening I quickly asked, "How much less coal, and how much would that coal be worth?" A few pocket calculators came out and a number was forthcoming. "And how much revenue is the customer losing because of the diminished output?"

By now I'm sure you've guessed what I was hoping. The savings were a near trade-off for the loss, providing an avenue of approach in discussing the problem with the utility.

I will always remember the joy of turning this negative into a positive (or at least defusing it to a stand-off), so much so that I refer to it as the "coal versus kilowatts" caper.

In this case the negative involved the situation. What can you do if the audience itself is negative? Sometimes you can turn objections around by using the "feel . . . felt. . . found" formula. In other words, "I can see why you might *feel* that way. . . . I've often *felt* that way myself. . . . But after studying all the possibilities, here's what I *found*. . . ."

I'm sure you've heard of "win-lose" situations where in selling a product or idea there's no gain if you give up and the customer wins, nor is there any long-term gain if you beat the customer into the ground and he signs just to get rid of you. The real sale is a "win-win" situation in which customers feel you understand them and their situations and can help them solve their problems.

You can't arrive at the win-win point by telling customers they are wrong. You might get there by the Socratic approach, wherein you ask a series of questions that have to be answered in the affirmative, leading to the final, big "Yes" that you are seeking. You might also make a series of suggestions and let the customer arrive at a conclusion. Perhaps you can provide two alternatives, each of which accomplishes your objective. If the customers have complaints, hold back on your reply until you are certain that you have all the information you can get, and they've gotten the complaints off their chests. And, be ready to concede minor points, while hoping to win the big one. Be careful not to rob your customers of their sense of control.

Psychiatrists and counselors use similar techniques where they let you arrive at solutions to problems with their guidance. Would-be sellers would do well to study their patience.

Above all else, when a program has problems (cost, schedule, performance), play it straight and be honest. As Mark Twain said, "You've got a lot less to remember when you tell the truth." Honesty, truth, and sincerity are head-and-shoulders above style, pizzazz, and slickness in sales techniques.

SELLING COMPLEX PRODUCTS, PROJECTS, OR PROGRAMS

The world we live in becomes more sophisticated every day. So much so that the scientists, technicians, or other experts are the only credible salespeople in some situations and must therefore do their own selling. The technical presentation actually becomes the point of sale as they try to convince an audience (of one or many) to buy their products or services, or to entertain further proposals or demonstrations. In this situation, a number of problems arise:

1. Usually, the audience will have seen many such presentations. Indeed, they may have already seen a similar one on that same day.
2. The "expert" giving the presentation has spent most of his or her career learning the technical expertise and may lack the interpersonal polish referred to earlier.
3. Because they are the experts, they occasionally engage in displays of technical arrogance in front of customers who have the same, or almost the same, level of expertise.
4. They feel that good technical work will sell itself. They deal in functions and features, and neglect to sell the benefits.

The Functions, Features, and Benefits Approach

The *function* of an item is what it does, and knowing what it does helps the customer to understand what it is. *Features* are the technical gee-whizzes that allow the item to perform its task. Features help customers to understand how it works, and that can be fairly interesting. But *benefits* are what it does for *them*, and that's the real payoff. Customers are interested in:

- Cost. (Will it save them money?)
- Schedule/Time. (Can they get it more quickly? Is it faster?)
- Performance. (Is it better? More reliable?)

Expressing features as benefits gives them the wallop they need to become vivid and forceful. Don't talk in vague, general theories; talk specifics. Don't sell radial tires; sell improved mileage, durability, and all-weather road handling. Don't sell aluminum siding; sell maintenance-free exteriors. Don't sell a ten percent cost reduction; sell a million dollars saved. To get customers to turn loose with their cash, show how the benefits of your approach outweigh the cost. This can be in terms of dollars or time saved, or perhaps the customers' own reputations. Do you have better service? Better financing? What do you have to offer that's better? Before customers stick their necks out, they have to know what's in it for them. Otherwise, their tendency will be to say no, to play it safe. Find a way for them to minimize any risks involved.

"AND, IN CONCLUSION . . ."

No book on selling would be complete without covering the *close*, and so it is with this chapter. You might be inclined to think of the last sentence or two of your talk in terms of something that might produce applause. That would be nice, *if applause is the result you are after.* But in the business world, you are more likely to have other types of approval in mind.

You are more likely to be seeking money or other resources, permission to present your ideas at the next level, a signature, a request for a proposal, or some other form of commitment from your customer or management.

So, you will want to do two things:

- First, summarize your benefits, conclusions, or recommendations. (Many briefers assume these are obvious after the logical buildup. *They are not.*)
- Then, "ASK FOR THE ORDER!"

Be Sure You "Ask for the Order"

Picture the timid door-to-door seller who presents the product, says, "Thank you," turns, and walks back down the path hoping the prospect will call out "Wait!" What do you think the chances of making a sale under those circumstances would be?

Some of us are so afraid of rejection that we never ask for the order, reducing the probability for either a "yes" or a "no" answer to zero. Asking would at least raise the odds to fifty-fifty. And, by meeting objections, stressing benefits, and providing favorable alternatives, we can tip the balance further and further in our direction.

The worst thing about not asking for the order is that the audience may think you are seeking advice or hand-holding as opposed to endorsement or resources. (Even worse, they may subconsciously hope you won't ask for action on their part. The response may call for fortitude, which might be in short supply.) Be sure they know what you want.

Don't Demand Immediate Results

An immediate O.K. is nice, but if you don't get it, don't push too hard. To do so may class you as the door-to-door type who says, "In order to get this fantastic bargain, you will have to sign up tonight." Don't substitute pressure for persistence.

Instead, you might ask, "Is there anything else you would like to know in order to help you consider this plan?" Or, "When could I check back with you?" Better still, "Can I check back with you in a week?"

If the door is still open a crack, you will probably know it. Perhaps the audience will ask for a copy of your visuals. (Aren't you glad you brought a hard copy? You will be even gladder if you have gone a step further and turned your visuals into a nice little booklet with a typed narration.)

One technique in selling is called the "Ben Franklin Close." In it, the salesperson lists all the reasons why it's a good buying decision on one side of the paper, and asks the prospect to list the reasons why it isn't on the other. The object of course is for the prospect to be unable to list any reasons for not buying, thus leading to a quick close. Although this technique has some high-pressure overtones, it can be useful if you see you are not going to be able to "close the sale." For example, you can fill in the plus side, leaving the minus side blank and ask for a chance to check back in a few weeks.

A friend of mine in the advertising business says he never tries to confront the customer with a yes or no decision. He feels most people find it more comfortable to make either-or choices. With the either-or path, the presenter can take the customer "down the beam" through a series of electives to a yes decision. Selling a single ad approach is a lot tougher than asking the audience, "Do you prefer this or that?"

If you still leave without an answer, review why you didn't get one, make the necessary adjustments, and follow up. Don't underestimate the power of persistence. In many forms of selling it takes at least five calls to get an order. And in some, five years may even be required.

Sometimes you will have a great idea and it just won't sell. If it doesn't sell in Indianapolis, save it for Fort Wayne. Another time, another place, another audience, and it may become the greatest idea since sliced bread.

Keep your chin up. Keep trying. Remember some of the things talked about here. As a result you won't have to knock your competition; you'll beat the hell out of them!

CHAPTER SEVEN

Practice Makes Perfect

THE SCENE IS Denver's Stapleton Airport. Not much can be seen through the cockpit windows except the swirling snow and the runway lights just beyond. Clearance received, the jet lumbers forward as the first officer advances the throttles. V_1 . . . V_2. The aircraft is rotated. Lifts off. Everything is normal—for a short while. Then the signals come. Loss of power from number two. Icing. The stick shaker warns of an imminent stall. The turn and bank indicator begins to roll over, and the altimeter winds down crazily until it suddenly stops at zero. Silence.

The cockpit door swings open. "Cuppa coffee, anyone?" asks the instructor, and a discussion ensues with the two pilots who have just "crashed" the simulator. Their conversation centers on what might have been done differently in a real-life situation and ends with an encouraging "Oh well, practice makes perfect," from the instructor.

Practice makes perfect in presentations too. Some experts recommend practicing a talk ten times before you give it. I wouldn't disagree, but I would like to differentiate between the terms practice, dry run, and rehearsal:

- *Practice* is something you can do alone, going over the talk "in front of your bathroom mirror" or into a tape recorder.
- *Dry run* is your first attempt in front of live people—some associates or members of your family.
- *Rehearsal* is that final run-through which will simulate the actual presentation as closely as possible.

There will be more on each of these terms later. But first a few words on their importance.

Many people don't take pains in preparing their presentations.

And their sloppy presentations are an insult to the audience who must suffer through them. I've sat next to these individuals on airplanes as they arranged their slides and lamely cracked, "Don't want to peak too soon!"

On the good side, I've seen preparations for major corporate presentations start four months in advance. In another case, I've seen an engineering manager and a manufacturing manager interlace their presentations so that one would not be a repetition of the information covered in the other. The two of them practiced together every day at lunch for two weeks, so that the result would be a smooth conversational dialogue.

How much time should you spend practicing? Chapter 1 suggested that the length of your talk multiplied by the number of people in the audience is a fair amount of preparation. Or, if that doesn't seem adequate, allow *one hour of preparation for every minute you plan to talk.* Take heart. Keep in mind that you've already accounted for many of those hours during the planning, organizing, and developing process. Also, you'll be breaking up the remaining hours into separate sessions, starting with practicing on your own.

PRACTICING ON YOUR OWN

As you read over your presentation you'll find little things that will make it clearer, sharper, and more colorful. You'll find new angles from which to approach your subject. You'll start polishing those rough edges. You'll develop new and better ways of saying things. And you'll begin to feel comfortable with your material.

Earlier, I mentioned practicing in front of your bathroom mirror, and I put it in quotes because of the number of "bathroom mirror" jokes on the lecture circuit. But why not in front of the mirror? Or in the shower? Or while riding to work? You can practice almost anywhere. Practice a little bit every day to avoid last-minute cramming.

Initially you'll be practicing with the script you've prepared. As you read the script, try to read it with your ear rather than your eye. Better still, read it aloud, underlining those words or phrases you want to punch up. Put in slash marks for pauses. Put parentheses around softer items. Knock out any tongue twisters. You may be able to handle, "Peter Piper picked a peck of pickled peppers" on the printed page, but it's tough to do in front of an audience.

Now find a tape recorder and record your presentation. By now

I'm sure most of you have heard a playback of your voices. The first time we are exposed to the sound of our voices most of us are somewhat shocked and don't like what we hear, not necessarily because it sounds bad, but simply because it's so different from what we hear inside our own heads.

Once you've gotten over this "Hey, is that really me?" aspect, you can lean back, close your eyes, and listen. Listen for changes in volume. Listen for changes in speed. Listen for changes in tone. Every speech instructor or book warns against speaking in a *monotone*. Concentrate on that word as it appears on this page: Drop the *e* and add a few letters and you have *monotonous*.

A good musician could probably listen to a talk and convert it to sheet music by marking the pace, volume, and tone. Words like *good*, *high*, and *expensive* would be slightly higher on the scale than their neighbors; while *bad*, *low*, and *cheap* would be lower. Some words (e.g., *other*, *impossible*, *uncomfortable*) would be stretched out for emphasis. Generally, tempo would be linked to intensity. Slow passages would be done in a softer voice and faster passages louder. Delivered properly, the talk would truly be music to the audience's ears.

Getting back to your talk, how did it sound? Harmonious or discordant? Most likely somewhere in between. Rewind the tape. Take out the script. Push *play*, and mark those passages that sound off-key. Change—replay—change.

With some tape recorders you can do a pretty good job of dubbing in the new material right over the old. The results may be a little bit patchy, but you'll have the added psychological advantage of wiping out the bad and replacing it with the good. This will also help you get away from relying on your script.

FOUR WAYS TO GIVE YOUR TALK

You are almost ready for your dry run, but first there's an important decision you have to make, which will become increasingly important as you get closer to the actual talk. The question is: "How do you plan to give your presentation?" The four basic approaches are:

- Reading
- Memorizing
- Impromptu
- Extemporaneous

Each has its advantages and disadvantages, so the question is which one will work best for you. Above all else, you should pick an approach you will be comfortable with.

To Read or Not to Read? That Is the Question.

There are times when you must read a talk. For example: when there are legal implications; when the press is present and you must be quoted accurately; in the case of a high-level executive, where someone else prepared the speech and you haven't had much time to review it; or because you are *absolutely* sure you can not do it any other way.

Why all these provisos? Well, quite simply, because reading a speech is not a good way to capture your audience. I know a few authorities will take exception to this, but most of them earn their livings as professional speech writers and deal with a clientele quite different from the average person reading this book.

The talk that is read to an audience is usually a downer. Shortly after, "Good morning ladies and gentlemen," the speaker's eyes leave the audience and shift down to the typewritten page. And, for the most part, the eyes stay down until the speaker reaches, "Thank you. Are there any questions?"

In brief, speeches that are read:

- Can insult the audience (they could read it to themselves better and faster).
- Sound artificial (the unnaturalness may be taken as insincerity).
- Are usually not tailored to the particular audience (certainly they lack flexibility to follow the lead of the audience as reflected by questions or interruptions).
- Need lots of practice to do well (they may not be the time-saver many people think they are).
- Represent indirect communication (the "authority" is in the script rather than in the speaker).

In spite of the foregoing, you may still be determined to read your talk. My job now becomes one of helping you look like you're not reading it.

If you decide to read a prepared speech, be sure you've "thought it out" thoroughly in advance. Otherwise, you'll just be reading something, with the chance of making a gross error. Think about what you are going to say, what it means, and how you are going to say it.

A "read" speech should be *read*, and *read*, and *read again* before it is ever presented. You must know a speech so well that you only have to look down occasionally. Otherwise you're trapped behind the lectern. This minimizes eye contact, and thus minimizes rapport.

Written humor or personal incidents are hard to handle in a read speech. Learn the gist of the story, not the words. Then wing it. Don't just see the words, see the images the words represent.

Most of us have seen Walter Cronkite on TV. (Cronkite was once cited as the most trusted man in America.) Cronkite "read" but it didn't look like it. You've got a lot more time to prepare than Cronkite did on the evening news, so theoretically you should be able to do better. Cronkite did have some other advantages such as his God-given talents and a teleprompter, so you're going to have to do some extra work to make up for that.

A good typing job can help make up for the lack of a teleprompter. Chapter 4 gave you some ideas on how to type your script. Here are some tips on how to mark it:

- Use colored pens for visibility.
- Put slash marks where you want to pause.
- Write "slow" between paragraphs.
- Use large, colored asterisks for slide changes.
- <u>Underline</u> for emphasis.
- Enlarge unusual punctuation (e.g., exclamation points or question marks).
- Circle words or phrases that need to be tied together.
- Mark gestures.
- Box passages you can memorize so you can give them looking up at the audience.
- And, having said all this, don't overmark. You could get lost.

In some cases you may be supplied with a prepared speech written by your organization—perhaps at company headquarters a thousand miles away. Commonly referred to as "canned" talks, these presentations attempt to match every speaker and every audience. It's like equipping every baseball player on a team with the same type of glove or the same size bat, or using the same lineup regardless of the ballpark or the opposing pitcher. Don't be afraid to modify a "canned" talk (without changing the content, or course) to make it *your* speech. If they wanted all the presentations to be the same, they should have hired a famous star and made a movie. Finally, never apologize for having to read it, and never refer to the script as having been prepared by someone else. Never say, "According to what it says here . . .," or, "The figures they gave me . . ."

If you are going to read your talk, try these techniques:

- Try to look up as much as you look down. When you pause at the end of a paragraph, get that next sentence so you can give it looking up.
- Read as little as possible. Wing it on short, familiar passages. Slide your thumb down the side of the page at a pace that will enable you to glance down and find the right spot.
- Talk naturally, even it if means an occasional "tha" for "the" or "ah" for "a."
- Turn up the volume. (When your head goes down your chin constricts some of your throat muscles.)
- Place the script as high as possible on the lectern. Tape a strip of cardboard or a pencil on the lectern. The higher you place the script, the higher your eyes and voice will be!
- Don't lean on the lectern; it's for notes to rest on, not you. Picture a sign on it that says "Wet Paint."
- Let the audience know you're not a clothing store mannequin with a recording inside. Gesture. Step away from the lectern to field questions or repeat key ideas.
- "Hide" the manuscript. Have it up there in advance so that your listeners won't think "God, do we have to sit through all that?" as you walk toward the lectern. (When I go to my dentist, I never see the novocaine needle, and I like it that way.)
- Don't staple your pages or turn them over. Slide them to the left and you'll avoid the hourglass effect mentioned in Chapter 4.

Memorization—The Robotic Approach

Memorized talks suffer from some of the same disadvantages as read talks. Memorizing is another form of reading—reading from within. Instead of the speaker's eyes being cast downward, they're turned inward like Little Orphan Annie's. Or as Pogo used to say, "All blunk out." They're turned inward because they are searching the speaker's brain for the next word or phrase that's supposed to come out, and when they don't find it—"Th-th-th-that's all f-f-folks."

You probably won't have the amount of time it would take to get a long talk down cold. Nor are you likely to give that talk enough times to make all that effort worthwhile. Furthermore, memorizing eliminates any spontaneity, resulting in a canned talk. "Was that live or on tape?" may be a great slogan for advertising recording tapes, but it's a bad question to leave in an audience's mind.

Impromptu Speeches

Impromptu speeches are given on the spur of the moment without any previous thought or preparation. They call for some pretty fancy tap dancing, and the only things that can help you are your own God-given talents, experience on the particular subject, and expertise gained in previous presentations.

Obviously, impromptu talks will take on an informal, conversational, flexible, and (if the speaker has everything under control) relaxed air.

Impromptu speaking is a special skill that is seldom seen. The best impromptu speeches I have ever given have been to traffic cops. The best impromptu speech I ever heard was by Dr. Gordon Lippitt of Organizational Renewal, Incorporated in Washington, D.C. Dr. Lippitt was a poor man's Jonathan Winters as he grabbed a few markers and began drawing diagrams while presenting his topic. I was so impressed I went to hear him a few weeks later. As a matter of fact I drove through a snowstorm to see what kind of impromptu talk he would give this time, and he gave essentially the same "impromptu" speech I had heard previously. At first I felt as though Lippitt might be putting something over on his audiences. Later I realized what a good speaker he actually is. He has the skill to mix in stories, illustrations, and examples spontaneously. The correct term for what he did is "extemporaneous."

Be Extemporaneous, Go with the Flow

An extemporaneous speech is one that is well-planned, thoroughly rehearsed, but not memorized word for word. Therefore it has all the advantages of an impromptu speech and none of the disadvantages of a read or memorized speech. You may have written the talk out as part of the mental process in preparation, but that script is not up there on the lectern, nor have you memorized it. What is up there are a few notes on your opening and closing, some catch phrases or key statistics, and a listing of the five or so main points you want to make in the order you want to make them. All of which you probably have memorized anyway. (Memorizing your opening and closing is a good idea to make sure they go smoothly, but in between you will be winging it.)

The benefits are enormous:

- This type of presentation allows you to adapt instantly to different circumstances.
- No matter how many times you give the presentation, it will have an air of spontaneity.
- Audience involvement and interaction are encouraged and can be handled without disruption.
- Your talks will be more dynamic and more interesting.

The audience will sense all of this and stay with you more easily. You'll be at one with the audience instead of merely spouting out read or memorized words. The more they feel you are talking *with* them, reaching into your own gut for the next thought, the better your talk will be received.

Asking speakers without experience to adopt this approach may be like asking the lame to throw away their crutches (the manuscript) without a trip to Lourdes, but be brave. The extemporaneous talk can be easier than you think.

First, you must have done your homework, but that's the case in any presentation. And the more homework you've done, the greater your confidence will be. Besides, you're the expert. Otherwise someone else would have been asked to give the talk. So try it. Give the extemporaneous talk a try at your dry run, relying on your script only when necessary. Chances are you won't be one-hundred percent satisfied, but stick with it. Use the tape recorder. Listen to it several times. Try it extemporaneously again at your dress rehearsal. Then make your final decision. Once you pull it off, you'll never go back to reading or memorization.

One of the biggest concerns in giving an extemporaneous talk is the fear of leaving something out. But that's not as bad as it seems. So you leave something out. Who's going to know? You will, of course, but the audience doesn't know what was supposed to be there. Chances are it's not really that important anyway, and if it is you can work it back in during the summary. Or, perhaps a confederate (or anyone else for that matter) will take notice and bring it up during the questions and answers.

In addition to brief notes on the lectern, there are many techniques to help you remember key points. If you're using flip charts, you can pencil in "stage whispers" along the side on which you will be standing. These are notes written lightly and small enough that only you can read them. They provide a safety net, there in case you need it. Viewgraph presentations provide an opportunity to put your notes directly on the viewgraph frames.

There are other techniques to help you remember the order of your talk. Some speakers like to picture a totem pole or stack of "groceries" and progress from top to bottom or vice versa. For longer talks I use a memory exercise I learned years ago in a Dale Carnegie course. It revolves around association. To be able to use it, you must first memorize a series of words that sound like the numbers they represent. For example, *one* sounds like *run*, *two* like *zoo*, *three-tree*, and so forth. As you can gather from the table below, this is quite easy, particularly if you limit yourself to numbers one through ten the first few times you use this technique. Use the words given in the table, or make up your own. The key words are then expanded into a mental picture and the topic or object to be talked about is then included in that picture. (The more

KEY-WORD MEMORIZATION TECHNIQUE

ORDER	KEY WORD	MENTAL PICTURE
1.	Run	Picture the Olympic runner racing across the fields, but instead of the torch in his upraised hand there's a _____. Or the runner is Mr. _____. Or he's at a specific location.
2.	Zoo	Picture the bears in their cage at the zoo and include the unusual object, person, situation, etc.
3.	Tree	Picture a tree, but instead of apples or oranges hanging from its branches, there's _____, or it's in a strange place.
4.	Door	Picture a revolving door, and every time it revolves it pushes more of something out into the street. Or a person exits. Or it's in a strange place.
5.	Beehive	Picture a beehive. But instead of bees coming out, bombers circle up into the air. Their bomb-bay doors open and out drops _____.
6.	Sick	Picture a hospital room. The nurse approaches the bed to give an injection, pulls back the covers, and finds _____.
7.	Heaven	Picture the angels up in heaven. In this case they aren't playing their harps, they're _____. Or maybe they aren't angels but _____.
8.	Gate	Picture a railroad crossing gate. It drops down in front of your car and there hanging or sitting on it is _____.
9.	Wine	Picture a bottle of wine that has tipped over on a table. The wine flows to the edge, drops over the side, and falls on _____. Or instead of wine, _____ flows out of the bottle.

ridiculous, the better.) For example, let's suppose the seventh item you want to talk about is the Accounting Department headed by Mr. Clark. Since seven stands for heaven, you would picture him and his winged associates playing harps. Or, if the narration involved computers, have the winged Mr. Clark and crew gathered around the latest model. Using this technique you can cover twenty topics with few or no notes. It can keep you going for at least half an hour. Another beauty of this technique is that if the audience wants to jump around from topic to topic, you can mentally cross each topic off as it is covered and go back to those that haven't been discussed. Yes, it seems complicated and it does take some practice, but you can do it. For practice, try it as a game with the family, asking them to pick numbers at random and

KEY-WORD MEMORIZATION TECHNIQUE

ORDER	KEY WORD	MENTAL PICTURE
10.	Den	Picture an animal den back in the woods. You enter the den hoping to catch the fox or whatever, and instead find _____.
11.	Football Eleven	Picture the quarterback in the huddle explaining the next play. Something's unusual, and it's _____.
12.	Shelve	Picture row upon row of shelves in _____, or holding _____.
13.	Hurting	Something is really *hurting* you. It's _____.
14.	Courting	You and your lover are "courting" in an unusual place or situation, or with a strange object.
15.	Lifting	You are straining to lift something which is terribly heavy because _____.
16.	Sickening	You are licking something very distasteful. What is it?
17.	Leavening	Picture a baker kneading some dough. There in the middle of the mess is _____.
18.	Waiting	You're standing at a bus stop waiting for _____, or sitting on a _____, or holding a _____, or standing next to _____.
19.	Pining	You are pining for your loved one or an object you desire. Picture an ornate, gilded picture frame that contains a photo of _____.
20.	Horn of Plenty	Picture the Cornucopia or horn of plenty. But, instead of overflowing with fruits and flowers it's _____. Or, the fruits and flowers are spilling out onto _____.

Courtesy of Dale Carnegie and Associates, Inc.

household objects to go with them. You'll amaze them as you rattle off the numbers and objects in the correct order. When you get it down pat, practice it in airports when the weather gets bad. You'll never have to buy another drink again.

THE DRY RUN

You are now ready to try out your ideas on others. Supposedly, mankind's greatest achievement is our ability to transmit ideas. At the same time, our greatest illusion is that we are transmitting the ideas we think we are, all of which becomes obvious in the dry run. *Everyone* hates dry runs. But, please, don't skip this step. If you do, you'll regret it!

A week or more before your talk, gather a few of your business associates, members of your family, or friends who have volunteered to review your presentations. Tell them what you hope to accomplish when you give the talk to the real audience, and who that audience will be in terms of backgrounds, education, and interests. Tell them how much time you will have. Ask someone to keep time as you do the dry run of your talk. And ask them to role-play as the intended audience and ask questions that might occur to them. Then give the talk, and as you do so, show rough sketches of any visuals you plan to use in the finished presentation.

If there are no questions, ask for them. And be prepared to wait until some are forthcoming. Don't forget how important it is to practice answering potential questions that may arise during your real presentation. Frequently the questions and answers are more important than the talk itself.

You will also be questioning your volunteer audience. Were they able to follow your talk? Did the benefits come across? Did you say anything you shouldn't have? Did you accomplish your stated objective? If they were giving the talk, what would they do differently? How did you do on the allocated time? Were there mispronunciations?

An error in pronunciation can have the same effect on an audience as scraping your fingers across a blackboard. It distracts them and may lead the audience to question your education and intelligence. Right now your pronunciation is probably ninety-five percent correct. But you need to work on that other five percent. Are you saying *fill um* for *film*, or *bag* for *beg*? Notice that we are not condemning accents. Accents can add flavor to a talk. (Indeed one major spice company has selected *Accent* as a trade name for a flavor enhancer.) Your accent makes you different from the next speaker and adds interest to your talk.

Dry runs are usually horrible, but that's good! They give you a chance to repair defects that weren't visible when you were practicing alone. Just one word of caution: Groups that review presentations are sometimes referred to as "murder boards," implying the hurt they can inflict. To avoid this situation, impose a few ground rules before giving your dry run:

- Select individuals who will give "constructive" criticism.
- Ask your volunteers not to interrupt the presentation for analysis or critique of a particular point. ("Real-life" questions are welcome.)
- You're interested *first* in what they liked, and second in what they would do differently.
- Since you're interested in perfection, no point is too small to mention.

Lick your wounds. Take every comment seriously, and if time permits, schedule another dry run.

FINALLY, THE DRESS REHEARSAL

You have now reached the third, and final, step in the practice/dry run/rehearsal cycle. With all the effort you've put into the first two, there may be an inclination to skip this step. Don't do it! *There is always a rehearsal. Unfortunately, it is sometimes in front of the real audience!* A professional performer would never think of appearing without rehearsing—Why should an amateur?

This chapter began with a flight simulator where every possible step had been taken to duplicate actual conditions. So it should be with your rehearsal. Try to hold it in the same place, at the same time of day, and using the same equipment as your actual talk. No point is too small, even what you plan to wear. After all, this is a *dress* rehearsal!

Now That You've Considered Their Ears, Go to Work on Their Eyes

In addition to capturing the interest of your audience's ears, you'll want to be capturing their eyes as well. Chapter 5 talked about all the various types of visual aids you could use to support your talk. Whatever type you picked, one thing will always be true: *YOU ARE*

YOUR MOST IMPORTANT VISUAL. You and what you are wearing will be in the audience's view far longer than any of your visual aids.

Now, while there's still plenty of time to make adjustments, ask yourself, "How am I going to look to that audience?" Your clothes are the frame. You are the picture.

The fundamental rule is dress for the audience. In some situations that might mean a hardhat and workshoes. As a general rule, it usually doesn't hurt to look affluent, but never dress flashily. Conservatively well-dressed is the goal. Ten minutes after you've gone, the audience should have forgotten what you were wearing. But if they were asked, they should agree that you were well-dressed. Usually that means conservative dress and solid colors. Save the checked pants for the golf course. John T. Molloy, author of *Dress for Success*, has made a career out of studying the impact of dress on business situations. In his book, he claims to be able to rate the success of sales personnel simply by observing how they are dressed.

Are your clothes out of style? How about your hairstyle? Even eyeglasses have become a fashion item for men as well as for women. Being drastically out of style can make an audience think you haven't had a new idea in ten years. How old is what you'll be wearing? Might this be a good time to purchase some new items? You'll probably be doing it before the year's end anyway.

I realize that some groups could care less about what you wear. And, I admit that the best talk I ever heard was given by an individual who couldn't afford a suit. But there are occasions that demand a certain level of dress, and for them I reserve a dark blue three-piece number I refer to as my "bank loan suit."

Women, of course, face their own problems in this area. Most of them are meticulous in their dress, yet quite a few complain of not being taken seriously by some of the males in their audiences. One young woman who voiced this concern was, unfortunately, presenting mixed messages to her listeners. Her dress, jewelry, and hairstyle were suitable for the disco, but not for the speaking platform.

Another woman who works in research and development dresses as sloppily as she can. Needless to say, this too is a distraction. The "I'm just one of the good old boys" approach doesn't work for male or female speakers. The books suggested in the resources section at the end of this book will give women some help in this area, especially when you add in two considerations: the type of person you are, and the type of organization you are representing.

Timing—Be Sure to Quit While You're Ahead

The moment you begin, the meter starts ticking. And with each tick you're depleting your audience's supply of interest. You want to be sure to finish your talk before your listeners finish with you. Don't press your luck—keep it short. And if you finish early, use the extra time for questions and answers, not filler. You can spoil your entire presentation by dragging out the ending and introducing extraneous material. Know how and when you will close, and how you will make your exit.

Are time allotments sacred? Of course not, but if there's an established agenda, it becomes a "contract" between you and the audience. When you don't stick to the schedule, you're breaking the contract. Running over just before lunch or at the end of the day certainly won't win you any audience awards. Conversely, the speaker who runs out of time and then has to change slides so quickly you can't read them, and skips the closing, looks equally bad.

To prevent this, practice your timing during the dry run and dress rehearsal. Have a colleague signal you when there are five minutes, three minutes, and one minute remaining. It's nice to know that there are five minutes left, but it's even nicer to know where you should be at that point. So be sure to have these checkpoints marked in your script or on your visuals. With this approach you'll probably be able to stay within thirty seconds of the desired time.

Rehearse Using Your Visuals

It's amazing how much time speakers will spend preparing visuals and then neglect to try them out until it's time for the actual presentation. When you give your presentation, you will be interacting with your visuals, and you want everything to go as smoothly as possible. That takes practice. Here are some things to look for now:

Charts

- Be dynamic. Are there any opportunities to write or draw on charts as you talk?
- Will the progressive disclosures work? (Don't use too much tape to secure the coverups.)
- Do you see any use for a second easel to show more detail, to keep some visual showing while presentation continues on

the main chart pad, or to record comments from the group while the presentation progresses?

- Could you use a few blank charts to cover an impromptu discussion?
- When you're ready, bind (staple) all of your charts together as a single unit for alignment and to prevent individual sheets from slipping out of the gripper. Finally, add stage whispers, those *lightly* penciled notes written at an angle on the side you will be working from.

Overheads

- Is it better to use a pen or pencil as a pointer on the projector or do you want to move away from the projector toward the screen to get your body out of someone's way? (The former is usually, though not always, preferable.)
- Would it help to tape a cardboard "stop" strip or an empty frame to the top of the projector to serve as an alignment guide?
- Is there sufficient table space to separate the stack of unused viewgraphs from the used stack?
- Can you change viewgraphs easily and handle progressions smoothly? (Some experts recommend turning the lamp off during changes. Others place an index card, with tape serving as a hinge, over the projector head and flop it back and forth as a light valve. And some merely push the old viewgraph aside quickly as they move on to the next.)
- Should you have some blank viewgraphs and transparency pens on hand in case the need arises to improvise?

Special table designed to house overhead projector (3M Model 39)

Lightweight, portable overhead projector (3M Model 6202)

Slides

- Do you have your slides already loaded in a tray with your name on it so you won't have to waste time when you get there and possibly load some incorrectly? (How to load slides will be found in Chapter 8.)
- Are any of your slides poor quality? Is there any way you can work around using them?
- Are any slides on the screen far too long? Would inserting a blank slide help?

Rehearse the Questions and the Answers, Too

You've already gotten started on this technique as part of your dry run, but be sure to build it into your dress rehearsal as well. No one can predict exactly what questions your real audience will ask, but your reviewers can probably come close by framing some questions around areas of concern, possible misunderstandings, etc.

Study Chapter 10 for tips on how to field questions. Before you hold your rehearsal, let the reviewers know you want questions during your talk. Then ask for more at the end, and wait until you get some.

WATCH WHAT YOU SAY

As mentioned earlier, practicing with a tape recorder can improve the sound of your talk. Today video recorders are becoming more and more common, providing you with an opportunity to check both sight and sound. If your organization doesn't have one, a friend may, or (if budgets permit) there are rentals available. Video playback can give you just as valuable a critique as your volunteers. With it you can check:

- Gestures.
- Eye contact.
- Body language.
- Interaction with visuals.
- Voice.
- Maddening mannerisms.

These last afflict all of us to a certain degree. Some involve the voice, such as the frequent interjection of "ah," or the more modern (and more irritating) "y'know." Both of these bad habits can be the result of failure to pause at the proper place, or the compulsive need to keep on talking. Pauses help you and they help the audience. Your audience can think about what you've been saying; you can think about what you're going to say. But don't pause indiscriminately—make it at the end of a particular point.

Other maddening mannerisms involve the body, as in the case of a heel-toe rocker; or the hands, which might be tugging at a tie, nose, earlobe, earring, or each other. What a pity to have the hands form a distraction when they could be making meaningful gestures.

What to Do with Your Hands While Your Mouth Is Busy

Make your hands work for you, not against you. As you view the videotape, where are your hands? Are they *both* thrust into your pockets, jangling your keys and change so much that the mike is picking up a sound like a Good-Humor truck? (One hand in an empty pocket is okay, *occasionally.*) Are your hands clasped in front of you in the figleaf, or "God I feel naked up here," position? Behind you at parade rest? Or, are they tucked into crossed arms, signifying closed-mindedness? Are they grasping the edges of the lectern so tightly that your knuckles have turned white? (Instead, try one hand resting loosely on the lectern and the other used for effect.)

Videotaping rehearsals provides an "instant replay" for analysis.

If any of these postures make you so comfortable that you can't go on without them, your audiences will have to learn to live with them. But keep in mind that they are all unnatural positions. To find your natural hand position, stand in front of a full-length mirror and raise your arms straight out to each side until they reach shoulder height. Now just let them drop. They'll slap against your hips, bounce around, swing a little, and come to rest in a *natural* position. Try this about a dozen times until you become comfortable. (You might want to alert your family members in order to head off snide remarks.) Now you've got a basic stance from which to start gesturing.

Assume a natural position and gesture when you have something to say with your hands. For example:

Gesture	Message
Point	Shows direction; makes a point
Palms up	Giving or receiving Asking for help
Palms down	Rejecting
Palms facing audience, fingers up	STOP!
Chopping palm	Division
Clenched fist	Strength, anger
Shaking index finger	Warning
Nodding head up and down	Approval, positive
Shaking head side to side	Disapproval, negative
Changing sides on platform	Shift in subject
Moving toward audience	Meeting of minds, receptiveness

You're trying to capture your audience physically as well as psychologically and intellectually. Gestures can do that for you. Imagine the added effectiveness of a speaker shaking his head while stating, "Pilots *don't* like that." Even a raised eyebrow can be a gesture showing excitement over an idea, regardless of whether it's natural or contrived.

A few more thoughts on gestures:

- If you're using slides in a partially darkened room, gestures will not be quite as important during the talk. However, they can still be used during the question-and-answer portion.

- Don't attempt gestures until you get any nervousness under control.
- Don't make your gestures too theatrical—the audience will spot it every time.
- Don't repeat gestures too often. (Bobbing your head up and down repeatedly will make you look like one of those spring-necked dogs in the backseats of cars.)
- Get the timing right.

Don't be like the preacher who, giving a sermon, said, "When the call comes from up there (pointing up), I'm going to be ready to go." (By then his arm had dropped and he was pointing down.) His congregation broke up with laughter, leaving him wondering why.

Gestures can be language without the spoken word. Some years ago, as Louise Fletcher accepted the Oscar for her role as the head nurse in *One Flew Over the Cuckoo's Nest,* she closed with a brief thank you in sign language for her deaf parents. It was the most touching part of the evening. You might even want to turn the sound off during your video replay to see how your gestures fare.

The "Eyes" Have It!

Once I asked a leading executive what was the most important presentations skill he had ever mastered. The man was an excellent speaker, and had even appeared on network TV. So I was really interested in his answer. His reply, with just a little bit of tongue-in-cheek, "Learning to walk backwards." What he was referring to, of course, was avoiding turning his back on the audience and losing eye contact. (Within a few days after writing this chapter, I saw him leading a group of VIP's on a tour of his laboratories. Would you believe it? He actually was walking backwards!)

In presentations, good eye contact can be a plus for both the audience and the speaker. Obviously, it makes the audience feel they're being talked to sincerely and honestly as human beings the speaker cares about. For the speaker, eye contact increases effectiveness—and if done properly, it can also make the speaker more comfortable.

Good eye contact is more than just having your head up, looking at the forehead of someone in the first row or over the heads at the back of the room. Good eye contact is picking out an individual in the audience and talking *to that individual* until you come to a pause, shift in subject, or some other breakpoint—and then shifting to someone else.

Here is where the speaker comfort factor comes in. All through our lives we engage in one-on-one conversations, a much less frightening activity than talking publicly. Now you have a chance to do just that with a larger audience. Start with someone you already know in the audience, or with someone who at least looks friendly. Then move on to someone else. And don't neglect those people sitting in the corners. In those really tough presentations, eye contact can reduce a one-on-one-hundred situation to one-on-one.

Some speech classes use an exercise where everyone in the audience stands or keeps their hands in the air until they feel the speaker has established eye contact with them individually. You might imagine your audience doing the same.

I know one high-level executive who had a bad habit of "checking his shoeshine" in the middle of his talks. Not only would his head go down, but it would stay down for a considerable amount of time. At first the audience would assume he was searching for a thought, then they would wonder whether he was being completely honest with them, and finally they would lose interest. Fortunately, someone had the guts to call this to his attention and he corrected the problem—greatly increasing his effectiveness as a speaker.

Eye contact (or the lack of it) should be evident from watching the videotape, particularly if you are using visuals. How good a view of the back of your head did you get as you moved to the screen or charts? I've seen quite a few videotapes of speakers carrying on long conversations with their visuals rather than with the audience. Pretty amusing in a dry run or dress rehearsal, but not so funny in real presentations.

By now you should be so familiar with what's on your visuals that you shouldn't have to read them to yourself; and the type should be large enough so that you shouldn't have to read them to the audience either. If you are using a pointer, look at the visual just long enough to make sure it's pointing to the right spot, then regain eye contact with the audience.

Interaction with Your Visuals

In addition to avoiding talking to your visuals instead of the audience, there are a few other don'ts you can watch for on your videotape:

- Did you hide your visuals from the audience? Did your body

block anyone's vision? (This is particularly a problem with viewgraphs.)
- Did you change any visuals too quickly?
- Did you interrupt your speech to handle aids? (Make the transition from visual to visual by saying a few lead-in words as you make the change.)
- Did your visuals and narration combine to present the same point or were there any mixed messages?
- Did you insult your audience by reading the visuals to them?
- Did you credit them with supernatural powers (show them a complicated visual while you engaged in equally complicated narration), or were you just trying to give them a choice as to which one to follow?

One other thing: All your visuals should be in final form for the dress rehearsal. But if you're missing one, don't try to *tell* the audience what it looks like, show them. Show them the butcher-paper chart or quickie viewgraph you prepared for the dry run. If it's a slide that's missing, insert a clear blank that you've written on with a transparency pen to give the main idea. Trying to explain missing visuals will throw your timing off and lead to other problems.

A Few Pointers on How to Use One

While I don't recommend the use of a finger, it's often better than many of the distractions caused by the use of pointers. Rather than use the pointer to give Papal blessings, practice your golf swing, or simply rap the charts or screen as a not-too-subtle way of saying, "Wake up, stupid," there are two simple rules for using pointers:

1. Point to something long enough so that everyone in the audience has had a chance to locate it. (Three seconds should be long enough.)
2. The rest of the time put the pointer down or keep it at your side out of the way.

Other Benefits of Video

By now I'm sure you are sold on the benefits of video, but there are two more points I should highlight.

First there's the use of video to practice the eyeball-to-eyeball, one-on-one type of presentation where there's bound to be a lot of interaction. Find the right person to role-play the other individual and go at it. Perhaps you'll want to try this role-playing with a series of individuals—one each day.

Second, there's the use of video as a confidence builder. Sound strange? I hope you didn't expect to look like a television personality on the video playback. For one thing the lighting wasn't that good, and the camera was an inexpensive model. Besides, there wasn't any makeup. Seriously, aside from the star image, most people's presentations look pretty good on TV. The little mistakes that you know were there didn't show up (the audience doesn't see most mistakes either), nor did that little bit of nervousness. True, there were a few mechanical items and some of those maddening mannerisms, but you'll take care of those next time.

Finally, don't ignore TV and radio broadcasts. You learned to talk by imitating your parents, and you can learn to talk better by imitating those who do it as part of their professions. Watch how politicians, radio newscasters, and religious leaders use their voices to sustain interest. Tell yourself, "This person's good, and I'm going to learn at least one thing that I can use in my own talks."

ANALYZING YOUR TALK AND THOSE OF OTHER SPEAKERS

If there is a golden rule for analyzing other peoples' talks (and your own), it is *Build on strengths before you tear down weaknesses.* People in the behavioral modification field refer to this as positive reinforcement. Immediately after a dry run or dress rehearsal of your presentation, you want feedback from your volunteer observers and, if you have one, the video camera. You want to know:

1. *What did I do right?* That way you can do it more often. Use and reuse those things that work best for you. Build on your skills.
2. *What did I do wrong?* You need to be aware of areas for improvement. Don't worry if you can't completely eliminate a shortcoming. Look for ways to reduce it little by little.

Oral feedback from your review team is fine, but written comments are a good addition. On page 118, you'll find a presentation analysis form used in various presentation courses. Side A, at the top of the page, is completed as the presenter gives the talk and serves as a checklist for further discussion. (Notice the equal

PRESENTATION ANALYSIS

Presenter _____

Topic _____

Date _____

"I particularly liked..."	"If it were mine to do, I would..."

Presentation analysis form (Side A)

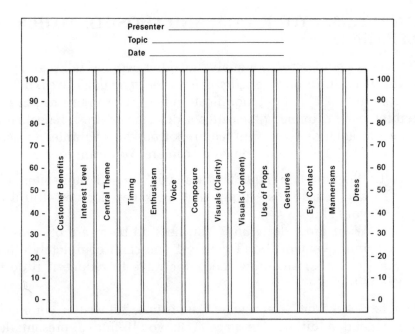

Presentation analysis form (Side B)

emphasis on strengths versus weaknesses.) Side B, below, covers a number of standard speech items and is quickly transformed into a series of bar charts simply by putting a horizontal line in each column at the appropriate level.

The form has many advantages. One is its anonymity. Although we hope none of your reviewers are going to write criticisms they wouldn't have the nerve to tell you, there are situations where a written point may be more tactful, such as where a fairly large group is present. Second, the form can save time, since it is quicker to read than sitting through an oral review where there are a large number of reviewers. The third, and most important, advantage of the form is its permanency. Collect the forms and save them. They can be looked at later as further preparation for this presentation or some future talk.

A FEW LAST WORDS

This has been one of the longest chapters in this book, and in real life it will be one of the areas where you should spend the most time.

You now have the confidence that comes from having done your homework. You know you can give the talk because by now you have already done so at least three times (and watched or heard it replayed three more).

You are now ready for the real thing. Surprisingly, it may be easier than your dry run and rehearsal. At least the audience won't be waiting to say, "If it were mine to do I would . . . "

CHAPTER EIGHT

Check
Your Rigging

WITHOUT A DOUBT, the greatest group of tightrope walkers in history was the Wallenda family headed by its patriarch, Carl. And, perhaps their greatest exploit occurred during a rehearsal one day at Madison Square Garden in New York City. With the entire troupe up on the wire on bicycles and balancing poles, a maintenance man inadvertantly turned off the main power switch leaving the family in total darkness forty feet above the arena floor. Summoning all the calm he could, Carl reassured his sons and daughters that things would soon right themselves, and fortunately he was correct.

Once I had the opportunity to see this great man in person. Despite his advanced years, Carl Wallenda still cut an impressive figure. But as imposing as he was, it was something he was doing that made a bigger impression on me. Here was the boss, the star, the patriarch, checking out the tautness of each wire in the myriad that connected to the main wire he would be walking on. It occurred to me that he could have told one of the roustabouts to do it, or asked a family member. But he had a good reason not to. They weren't going up on that wire—he was!

And so it is with talks and presentations. The next few pages cover all the things you need to check out ahead of time to make sure your performance is flawless. Many of them are minor and mechanical, and your audience may never notice; that is, of course, unless things go wrong. When that happens, you may or may not be as fortunate as the Wallendas were at Madison Square Garden.

When I cover the importance of checking your rigging with groups of meeting planners, I like to ask, "How many of you have ever been trampled by an elephant?" . . . "Nobody, I dare say. Well then, how many have been stung by a bee? Almost all, which just goes to prove it's the little things that can hurt you!"

Your attitude might well be, "I'm not a janitor or projectionist! I've got other things to think about. Let someone else handle the details." Not an unreasonable attitude except for one thing: you've got a vested interest in how well the presentation goes. It's your countless hours of research, writing, and rehearsal that have been invested—not the janitor's. And it's you and your reputation standing at the lectern—not the projectionist's.

Clearly, if you care about how you look and how well you communicate, the responsibility for the preliminary arrangements rests with you. Take a look at some of those important little things you need to do in advance of your talk.

BE AN EARLY BIRD

Given advance warning, most problems can be avoided in time. A week or so before your presentation you should be checking any printed material you plan to hand out and any props or models you plan to use. Are your visuals ready? Has the necessary projection or other audio visual equipment been reserved? Has the audience been notified as to time and place? Has the meeting room been set aside?

If possible, visit the room a week in advance. If you're using visual aids, you have both a good reason and a good excuse for doing this. Check seating, electrical outlets, and switches. Measure distances and screen size to determine the focal length of the lens you'll need. If you should happen to meet the custodian while you're there, offer a few kind words along with a diagram of the desired setup. This can work wonders later on.

Hopefully, wherever you speak you will have some help from local people in making suitable arrangements. But don't count on it! You can't walk in five minutes before you're due to go on and expect all to be in order. It just doesn't work that way. Murphy's Law makes sure of that. Plan to arrive about an hour before your audience is due. And make sure the chairperson, custodian, projectionist, and other appropriate people know you plan to arrive early so that:

- You'll be able to get into the room.
- There will be someone there to help you. (If in doubt, take a friend.)

- Others who are involved won't be operating on a last-minute rush.

Spend that hour checking all the mechanical aspects of your presentation. There's almost always something that needs to be done. And if, miraculously, all is to your satisfaction, then use part of the remaining time to glance through your script once more, and the rest to relax for a few moments and get in tune with the room. But before you relax, be sure you've covered *all* the bases!

WILL THE AUDIENCE BE COMFORTABLE?

Audience comfort generally revolves around two factors: heating and seating. Adjustments to the heating or air conditioning will take time (particularly with the newer locked thermostats that only the custodians or maintenance personnel can adjust), so proper temperature is one of the first things you will want to check for. If the room has only been open for a few minutes, it's understandable that it will be too hot or cold, but check the air coming out of the vents to make sure things are headed in the right direction.

Don't underestimate the importance of this obvious item. It could ruin your entire presentation. In Philadelphia, I once had the misfortune of giving a series of talks in a storeroom where the only heat was from plug-in, resistance-type electrical heaters. The wiring system in the room was so old that every time I added a slide projector, the load created by the heaters blew a fuse. Faced with this either-or situation, you can probably guess which option my frozen body selected.

In terms of seating, keep in mind the old adage, "The brain can only absorb as much as the buttocks will endure." Having an uncomfortable audience because of poor seating can provoke just as much negativism as poor temperature control. Chances are you will be severely limited in what you can do in this area, but here are a few suggestions:

- If you have any say about the room selected, consider the seating (along with ceiling height, overall dimensions, layout, screen location, etc.).
- If the meeting is important enough, perhaps better chairs can be substituted from another room.
- Remove any surplus seats (or stack them in the back of the room), culling out any seats that are damaged or of a different style.

Perhaps the biggest latitude you will have is in the arrangement of the seating, and this is no small item.

SEATING ARRANGEMENTS

If you're talking to a large audience in an auditorium, obviously there's not much to be done about arrangement. Auditorium seats can be "roped off" (with a roll of masking tape) to force a less-than-capacity crowd closer to you. In some auditoriums, this roping off effect can be enhanced by turning off the lighting in distant sectors.

Smaller groups and small rooms offer many options. Tailor the seating arrangement to fit the size of the group, the nature of your talk, and your personality. Various arrangements can stimulate or inhibit discussion. Here are a few you might want to consider:

Theater Style

Theater style offers the greatest number of seats in the smallest space. You might want to consider this setup for any group numbering over fifty, particularly if room size and screen size are limited. The lack of tables is disadvantageous in that your audience will have difficulty taking notes. They will also not have anything on which to rest their elbows. And row upon row of seating may

U-shaped seating promotes dialogue, as does
"lights-on" projection capability of overheads.

block the audience's view of you and/or your visuals, unless some sort of elevated platform is provided. Most formal theaters feature a stage, but if one isn't available, you can build your own out of "risers" if they are available from the maintenance personnel.

Classroom Style

While this setup won't handle as many people as the auditorium style because of the addition of tables or desks, it is still quite efficient in terms of capacity. The position of authority remains up front, which may be desirable. Classroom setups promote teacher/student discussion, but inhibit group discussion.

Classroom style is good for groups of thirty to fifty or more. At the higher end you might want to arrange the rows with a slight curve or slant (curving toward the speaker, as shown on page 125.)

U-Shaped Seating

Perhaps the best arrangement wherever both audience and room size allow, U-shaped seating is ideal for groups of fifteen to thirty. Attendees can all see each other, promoting group dynamics. Yet, the source of authority lies in the open end of the U presided over by the speaker and the visuals. This setup also allows the speaker to step into the audience by entering the open end.

When butting the tables together to form the U, it's generally better to put those forming the sides outside those forming the base of the U. This will provide a broader open area where room width allows. It will also provide a little more room up front for the speaker and the visuals.

Hollow (or Solid) Square, Board Room, or Circled Chairs

These circular arrangements are good in situations calling for shared leadership or teamwork. Theoretically, every seat is equal. This arrangement is excellent for groups up to a dozen. The tighter the circle, the less formal (and easier) the discussion will be.

Offset Seating

This arrangement places the speaker at the front corner of the audience instead of at the center. Its value lies in presentations involving overhead projection. It avoids the situation where the

Solid Square

Classroom or "Amphitheatre"

U-Shape/Outside Only

Standard seating arrangements

speaker has to step aside after placing each viewgraph on the projector so that the speaker's body will not block anyone's view. Careful setup and experimentation will be required to make this setup work to maximum efficiency.

Other Seating Arrangements

There are many other possibilities. For example, there's a V-shaped arrangement with the speaker at the point of the V. (No doubt who's the boss here!) There's also a T arrangement for banquets. If you come up with a variation that suits your purposes, give it a try.

Of course the best way to ensure arriving at an arrangement that will suit your purposes is to send a sketch ahead of time whenever practical. Some rearrangement is always possible upon arrival, but finding people who want to move furniture early in the morning or after the sun has gone down can be pretty difficult.

If you're at all technically inclined, try to draw your sketch to scale. Standard collapsible tables measure either 8 feet or 6 feet long by 15, 18, 24, or 30 inches wide. You'll want 3 feet between rows. Try to leave at least 12 feet between the front row and the wall for yourself, your screen, the lectern, chalkboard, easel, and a table for handouts, and indicate their position. Also indicate any projector stands or tables, plus tables for coffee or other refreshments.

When locating projectors, keep in mind that the cooling fans in some slide projectors are fairly loud. Therefore, it's a good idea to locate them behind your audience rather than between you and your audience. This will require a little extra room in the back, an elevated stand or two tables stacked atop one another, the right type of lens, and a remote-control extension long enough to reach the lectern, but it's well worth it in terms of reducing the noise and other distractions. Whatever the setup, never plan on placing your projector on the same table where people will be sitting. The slightest jiggle by anyone will make the image jump several inches on the screen.

Now, having drawn all of this, add a list of required items at the bottom of the page or on an accompanying page. If available, add water service (a pitcher and glasses on a tray with a cloth liner) and tablecloths for a touch of class. (Green, blue, or pastels will do nicely. Avoid white and red unless you serve breadsticks.) Ashtrays should, of course, be available and clean. (More and more larger meetings are being divided into smoking and non-smoking sections.)

Offset seating arrangements for overhead projection

As mentioned earlier, having seating arrangements spelled out in advance will certainly save a lot of time. If you are unable to do so, or nobody paid any attention to your arrangement, do what you can in the time available and move on to the other critical items. Key among these is the projection equipment.

PROJECTION EQUIPMENT

There are two things you will want to know as soon as possible about your projection equipment:

1. Is it there?
2. Does it work?

If you think these questions sound a little ridiculous, you've never had anyone say, "Nobody told me that we needed to order a slide projector." Nor have you ever been wiped out by a burned-out bulb left in a projector, or found that the lens or some other critical component was missing.

Be sure to project at least one of your visuals to see that:

- Your visual fills the screen without spilling over, and all lettering is as large and easy to read as possible. (The larger the screen, the better.)
- The image is positioned as high on the screen as possible, helping people to see over the heads of those in front. (Four-and-one-half feet from the bottom of the visual to the floor should be adequate. Using only horizontal visuals will also help.)
- The projector is focused properly.

Correctly loading slides in tray

- Images are rectangular. (If keystoning occurs, can it be reduced by tilting the top of the screen outward or pulling the bottom back?)
- None of the seats will have an obstructed view when you are at the lectern or overhead projector.
- Seats in the front row are not at too sharp an angle to the screen.

Unless you are really pressed for time, run through all your visuals for a quick review and make sure:

- The remote control is working properly.
- Nothing has been damaged in transit. (Slide frames can sometimes pop apart.)
- Everything is in the right order. (Not so much a problem with slides carried in a tray, unless there have been last minute changes—always a concern with viewgraphs.)
- Everything is right-side up. (There are eight possible ways to project a slide or viewgraph, making the odds seven-to-one against you if you leave it to chance. As a matter of fact, I once saw a speaker try more than eight times and still not get it right!)

It's really very easy. With slides, merely hold the slide above the tray, looking in the direction the projector's beam will follow. Now, when the slide is in the correct reading position, invert it as you "dunk" it into the tray. (See the illustrations on page 128.) Viewgraphs are even easier. If they are placed on the projector so they read correctly as you face the audience, they will read correctly on the screen.

LIGHTING

As part of your projector check, you will also want to familiarize yourself with the room's lighting controls. Does the room have a dimmer switch? Fantastic! A single off-on control spells trouble.

You can show viewgraphs in full light, but a slight dimming would be better. Slides will require some additional dimming, perhaps down to the level where people can see well enough to take notes. Movies will require even more dimming, but should not be shown in total darkness. With all of these, make sure the ceiling lights don't create any "hot spots" on your screen.

There are some things you can do with those lighting controls. If the room has a dimmer, experiment to find just the right level.

Then put a piece of masking tape on the wall or knob, marking the correct position so that you (or an associate) can return to it quickly.

No dimmer switch? Check to see if there are two on-off switches. If so, you are probably in luck. Each should control one-half of the room. Just leave the half where the screen is located turned off. Occasionally, you'll find two switches that work a bit differently. I once found two switches, each of which controlled every other bulb in a series of 150-watt bulbs spaced across the ceiling. At that wattage, having either switch off didn't make an appreciable difference. Ingenuity, however, coupled with a quick trip to a local store and a borrowed stepladder, saved the day. I substituted seven-and-one-half-watt bulbs throughout one of the circuits, thereby providing two (actually three if you want to be technical about it) levels of light, not unlike three-way bulbs.

But what if there is only one single wall switch? In that case, try to borrow some auxiliary lights to leave on while you turn out the overheads to show your visuals. A few table or floor lamps will do nicely. Or you can make that trip to the store again and pick up some nightlights. Get enough to plug one into each of the outlets.

Why all of this fuss about lighting? Well it's certainly more than just the fear that your audience might fall asleep if it's too dark. You want them to be able to take notes, see you (and vice versa), and feel comfortable asking a question.

There is one other aspect of lighting that should be touched on: windows. In addition to presenting a distraction, windows without drapes can present a lighting problem that is virtually impossible to overcome—unless you're willing to wait until dark. I once saw 500 people, intent on seeing a movie, head to a cafeteria where a handful were frantically trying to paste brown paper over thousands of square feet of windows because no one had alerted the janitorial force or checked to see that it had been done ahead of time. Another time, I went to England to give a slide presentation to a proposal team. It was a nice trip. Unfortunately, their quarters were new, and the blinds hadn't been installed. Fortunately, for some reason—probably uncertainty about available equipment—I decided to take viewgraphs as well as slides.

Learn to expect the unexpected!

GETTING THE FEEL OF THE "STAGE"

Once you've covered seating arrangements, projectors, and lighting, you should be up at the front of the room checking all the other details.

If there actually is a stage, practice climbing the stairs and moving around on it. I once almost walked (fell would have been more like it) off the front of a stage, which is one of the purposes of footlights and yet another good reason for not turning the house lights down too low.

Does the lectern have a light on it? Does it work? (The first time you try to look down at your notes is *not* the time to find out.) Does it contain any other light controls? Do you have any props or handouts to place inside the lectern? (The shelf under the lectern can be used to hide all sorts of things, not the least of which is a glass of water.) Where is the slide advance button? Is the height of the lectern adjustable? Some have pegs for adjustment, others operate electronically. A few lecterns come equipped with timers, but beware of the mechanical variety that are so noisy they can be heard in the third row.

Microphones

For any audience larger than fifty, you'll want to consider using a microphone. Over one hundred it's a must. Yes, I know they can hear you in the back row, but you're also breaking their eardrums in the front row. And if you're soft-spoken, you *really* need a microphone.

Microphones are delicate. Treat them with care. Despite their rugged appearance, they are the most sensitive element of any public address system. If nothing else, *never* blow into a microphone to test the system. Scratch the microphone lightly or snap your fingers in front of it to check it out. Better still, try a few "Test . . . one . . . two's" or a portion of your talk.

The basic rule of microphone use is to ignore it entirely and speak to the audience in a comfortable voice. Overcome the tendency to talk louder. With a well-adjusted public address (P.A.) system, you could talk forever without straining your vocal chords. It's also acceptable to ask your audience if they can hear you if you sense there are problems, then adjust your voice according to the response. Finally, don't stand too close to or lean into the mike. When you're too close, you can hear yourself through the P.A. system. Pull back to a position where you can't hear yourself through the system. That's about where you should be. (Eighteen to twenty inches should be about right.) If it's an uncomfortable position, then lower your volume (voice or amplifier) for the same effect.

Note that the mike works with your mouth, not your eyes. If it's positioned so high that it's aimed at eye level, lower it.

Lavaliere microphones give you greater freedom of movement—they're smaller, and easier to ignore. They are also a little trickier to use. The ones that attach with a clip are easy enough. Those that use a lanyard around your neck can present problems, the first of which occurs when the speaker attempts to slip the loop over his or her head without unhooking it. Usually the loop is too small, resulting in mussed hair, glasses knocked askew, and a lot of mike noise, including audible grunts as the speaker tries to force the loop down over the ears and nose.

The secret, of course, is to unhook the loop, which leads to the second problem. Not knowing exactly how to rehook the loop, speakers strain their necks, heads askew, so they can see what they are doing—a next-to-impossible task—all of which is usually unnecessary. Most lanyards operate on the ball-and-hook principle. The ball is at the free end of the cord, and the hook is part of the bracket that holds the cord to the microphone. Holding one in each hand, the speaker need only place the hook over any part of the cord and then slide it down the cord until it engages the ball. Voila! Whether attached by clip or lanyard, the lavaliere mike should be positioned over your *sternum*. (That's just above the solar plexus, not what you nautical types are thinking.)

Most lavaliere mikes are omnidirectional, thus *clothing rustle* can become a problem. To minimize this, grab the cord at arm's length and tuck the loop under your belt or into your waistband. If you are wearing one, your jacket will hide it. Now, body movement causes no cord or mike movement, hence no background noise. There's one other advantage: this technique provides an early warning when you literally reach the end of your rope, and prevents you from hanging yourself on stage. Think of the background noise that would cause!

Two final notes about the P.A. system:

1. Other than turning it on, try not to mess with someone else's system. The result can be trouble. Public address systems are often customized or may be preset for another (perhaps more important) event scheduled after your talk. If at all possible, have someone familiar with the system control it, or at least show you how.

2. If for any reason the sound system acts up during your talk, pause until it's fixed or turn it off and rely on your voice power. "Feedback," that ringing or squealing that has the same effect on the audience as scraping your fingernails across a blackboard, is to be avoided at all costs.

Modern sound systems are much more reliable than those of a few years ago. You may never have to use one, but if you do, don't become its slave. Try to forget it's there.

THE SPEAKER'S CHECKLIST

The previous paragraphs covered most of the major factors in checking your rigging. The table on pages 134-135 recapitulates these along with other odds and ends on a single sheet. You might want to make a copy to take with you on the day of your talk. Hopefully it will keep you from ever having to tell your audience, "Sorry, I didn't think of it" when something goes wrong, which is like saying you didn't think they were important enough.

THE SPEAKER'S EMERGENCY KIT

Although I was never trampled by an elephant in my speaking career, I did get stung by a lot of bees—so many that I was tempted to assemble an emergency kit that would take care of any possible difficulty. The contents are listed on pages 136-137, and I offer it to you as a once-in-a-lifetime opportunity to avoid those once-in-a-lifetime disasters. As you can see, the total contents would fill a three-suiter. If you're a professional meeting planner, get the model with wheels on it and take the whole nine yards. (Have you ever seen the inside of a paramedic's truck?) If you're an occasional speaker, pick a few items that you think will do you the most good. Someday you may have a chance to say, "Boy, am I glad I brought that!"

THE SPEAKER'S CHECKLIST

Room
Reserved in advance.
Floor plan sent in advance.
Temperature and ventilation.
Coatracks in "secure" location.
Clean up in advance.
Six square feet per attendee?
Excess chairs removed.
Will corner seats in front row be able to see screen clearly?
Adequate clear space up front for you and equipment.
Divide large groups into smoking and non-smoking.
Close blinds to eliminate distractions.
Must windows be blacked out?
Build speaker's platform with one-foot risers for larger groups.
Wastebasket, trash container.
Tape door latches for silence during late arrivals.
Table for handouts, etc.

Breaks
Refreshments scheduled.
Table for coffee, etc.
Wastebasket.
Restroom locations.
At least one break for every two hours (more frequently in afternoons).

Place Settings
Name tents, pencils, pads, water, ashtrays.
Broad felt-tipped markers for name tents (one for every three attendees).
Agenda for longer meetings.
Rolls of mints or candies.

Projector(s)
Who will supply projectors?
Tables or stands supplied.
Plugged in, aligned, and focused.
Any light fixtures in the way?
Lenses dust-free.
Spare bulbs on hand.
Takeup reel available for movie projector.
Extension cords taped to floor, outlets, and table legs.
Electrical circuits adequate to handle full load plus coffee urn, etc.
Remote control working properly.

Projectionist
Has marked script or cue sheet.
Has signal light or headphone buzzer.
If green, yellow, and red timing lights are used, agree on schedule.
Small light available for projectionist.

THE SPEAKER'S CHECKLIST (cont.)

Sound
Mike and speakers working.
Practice putting lavaliere mike on.
Feedback problems?
Check levels and set if required.
Do you want talk recorded?

Lighting
Adjustable?
Levels checked out and marked.
Who will work the lights?
Will auxiliary lights be required?
Windows adequately draped.

Signs
Room location sign in lobby or hall.
Meeting title on room door.
Message board for day-long sessions.
"Quiet Please—Meeting in Session."

Easel/Chalkboard
Fresh pad.
Fresh markers, varied colors.
Chalkboard clean.
Colored chalk.
Eraser.

Lectern
Light working?
Timer working? Noisy?
Water nearby.
Signal to projector/projectionist.
Pointer available.
Props hidden.
Script or cue sheet ready.
Height properly set.
Does it block anyone's view of screen?

Handouts
Arranged in order.
Conveniently located.
Evaluation forms or surveys.
Current reprints.
Where do you want handouts?
When will you distribute?

Screen
Large enough for readability.
High enough for visibility. (Bottom of
      screen should be 4½ feet above
      floor.)
Fill screen with image.
Does image keystone?
Any hot spots from overhead lights?
Offset for viewgraphs.

Visuals
In correct order.
All right-side up.
Extra blank viewgraph sheets.
Movies or videotapes advanced to
      proper start.
Sound levels set.

EMERGENCY KIT FOR PRESENTATIONS

Paper towels
Small box of pushpins
Plug adapter (3-prong to 2-prong converter)
Extension cord(s)
Extension for slide projector remote control
Roll of masking tape
Small roll of transparent tape on dispenser
One box of assorted markers
One dozen manila file folders (When open to 19 by 12 inches they
    make a good emergency chart.)
Transparency pens for writing on viewgraphs
One box of transparencies (black on yellow)
Soft chalk (white and colored)
Hand towel
Wet napkins
Eraser
Two collapsible pointers
Four nightlights (for rooms having only off-on lighting)
One 8½ by 11 meeting pad (with pen)
One pocket-sized memo pad (with pen)
One pack of 3 by 5 index cards
One calendar
Assortment of stomachache, headache, and cold or allergy relief
    medications
One box of throat lozenges
Various sizes of company logos
One corporate telephone directory
Small slide viewer or magnifying glass
One-half dozen translucent sheets that slides snap into (in case
    major rearrangement or sorting is required)
Matchbooks with company logo
White-out (for whiting out errors)
Single-edge razor blade
Scissors
Pocket knife
Two large clips (to hold charts in case easel is broken)
One dozen blank black slides
One dozen clear slides
Pocket flashlight
Cricket (for slide change where no other signal is available)
One dozen envelopes with stamps
One express-mail or package service envelope and form

EMERGENCY KIT, CONT'D

Shoeshine packs
Thirty pieces of 8½ by 11 white card stock to fold in half for
    name tents
Stick-on name badges
One dime (for removing jammed slide trays)
Small American flag (in case you are accused of "flag waving")

WHAT TO DO WHEN EVERYTHING'S UNDER CONTROL

The last thing that needs a little mechanical adjustment is *you*. Now is the time for that trip down the hall to straighten your tie, brush your hair, or whatever. If you tend to speak with your hand in your pocket, then empty the pocket of coins, keys, or anything else that will jangle and distract the audience. Also remove pens from outside coat or shirt pockets where they might cause a visual distraction. If you are to be introduced, go over the material with the chairperson—not only to catch any possible errors, but to force a rehearsal.

For some, this is a good time to relax, practice your mantra, or at least do a little deep breathing. For others, this is a time to get fired up, just as some football players do. In general, I would recommend the former for the less experienced speakers who might need to get some nervousness under control, and the latter for the old pros who may be a bit blasé.

Eve Zibart researched this area and wrote an interesting article for the *Washington Post*. According to Eve, here's what the stars do.

> Operatic soprano Renata Tebaldi had to have a portrait of her mother on her dressing room table . . . Roger Daltry of "The Who" runs in tight little circles backstage, around and around and then right out onto the stage . . . Jazz-rock bassist Stanley Clarke indulges in a personal kind of meditation . . . Country superstar Loretta Lynn has to go off entirely on her own . . . Tenor Joe Bonsall of the Oak Ridge Boys does calisthenics . . . Jim Lehrer (of the "MacNeil/Lehrer Report") says, "I must get up. *I get up.* The adrenalin flows . . . the alternative is just too horrible."[15]

Ah, I think the audience is arriving. Since you've got everything under control, it's a great opportunity to meet a few of them. They'll be impressed, and you won't feel like you're talking to a group of strangers.

CHAPTER NINE

It's
Showtime

SOMEWHERE, WHAT SEEMS a hundred or more miles away, you hear the words, " . . . and now, it brings me great pleasure to introduce . . . " Or, the voice more likely says something like, "Joe here has an idea that might increase productivity in the assembly area, and I asked him if he would go over it with us."

Whatever the introduction, within a few moments it will be your turn to be doing the talking to that "sea of upturned faces" that Sir Walter Scott wrote about. This chapter will take you through that experience, pointing out a few tips you can use the next time you do it for real.

BATTLING THOSE BUTTERFLIES

Everybody experiences a certain amount of anxiety when talking to a group. It's natural to have a higher pulse rate before starting a speech, because your adrenalin is flowing. It's an unfamiliar situation and you may feel somewhat out of control. Even the stars who will perform tonight on Broadway face this experience. They never know for sure what the response is going to be. So, the trick is not to eliminate nervousness, but to control it. There's nothing wrong with having butterflies in your stomach. It's when they get out and flutter around the room that hurts. Here are a few ways to keep them from escaping:

- Remember, you're the expert—even if your listeners all outrank you. If you didn't have something worthwhile to say, you wouldn't have asked (or been asked) to talk.

- Remember all the time and effort you've put into preparing. Knowing that you've done your homework should instill confidence.
- Remember that everyone in the audience (at least everyone who "counts") wants to learn from you, and wants you to succeed.
- Practice diaphragmatic breathing. Stand or sit up straight and provide more push from your diaphragm. Essentially this means taking deeper breaths. It pumps oxygen into your system and gets more oxygen to your brain. It also clears your lungs of stale air. (Most of us use only the top third of our lungs.)
- Loosen up. Before taking off in an airplane, the pilot wiggles the controls to make sure everything is going to work. Speakers should do the same thing. Don't sit there tight-jawed.
- Keep telling yourself, "I'm glad that I'm here, and I like what I'm doing . . . I'm Glad That I'm Here, And I Like What I'm Doing! . . . I'M GLAD THAT I'M HERE, AND I LIKE WHAT I'M DOING!!!"—*Even if it's a lie.*
- Be yourself. Nobody expects you to be a movie star or William Jennings Bryan. Remember all the rules, but do what's natural for you.

If you're still a little nervous, think of it this way. We practice "public speaking" every time we talk to someone. So pick out somebody who looks friendly and get ready to start talking.

THE HANDOFF—INTRODUCER TO SPEAKER

When you've been introduced, you should acknowledge the introduction. In a small group, a simple "Thank you, Sharon," with a bridge into the talk, such as, "You know, Sharon's right . . . " may suffice. With a larger group you might want to use the same words, but add a handshake as you pass each other on the stage or exchange places at the lectern. This provides both verbal and visual acknowledgment.

You may get an offbeat introduction such as, "It's been said that today's speaker needs no introduction. And if that isn't true I'm in one hell of a fix, 'cause I've never heard of him." If so, you might want to try a riposte used by former Vice-President Mondale. "Let me thank you for that wonderful introduction. Of all the introductions I've ever received, that was certainly the most recent!" Or you may get an overzealous introduction that goes on and on, in which case your opening remarks might be, "And, in conclusion . . . ," or, "Are there any questions?"

When you're introduced, look like you're happy and anxious to get started. Be close at hand, not in the back of the room. Rise promptly, move forward quickly. When you reach the lectern pause briefly and survey the audience. You've captured their attention, now hold it with good eye contact.

Start with a smile, even under pressure. Some experts say, "Smile until they smile back at you." When there's no smile, the audience withdraws.

NOW YOU'RE READY TO START, BUT IS THE AUDIENCE?

With larger groups there may be some housekeeping details that need to be taken care of, such as:

- *Calling for a stretch break.* Suppose they've been sitting there through an invocation, dinner, the "Pledge of Allegiance" and "God Bless America," recognition awards for almost everyone in attendance, and finally it's your turn. Even though the schedule may not call for one, you had better call for a stand-in-place stretch break. A few mild aerobics can be your best possible opening. You can start with, "Gee, it felt good to stand up. Why don't you join me for a moment?"
- *When "Please be seated" doesn't work.* Maybe they've just had a break and they're reluctant to reassemble. With small groups this usually doesn't cause many problems. Normally people will take their seats when asked. In larger groups, the mere process of finding the right seat and sitting down can take a fair amount of time, leaving you or the M.C. at the mike with nothing to say. Instead of just standing there or getting waspish, try a little humor. "They must not be able to hear me, I can't believe they're ignoring me" or, "If you don't sit down I'm going to start taking names."
- *Filling the front rows.* You're about ready to give your talk, but everybody is sitting in the back rows, with no one up front. If you ask them to move, no one may, leading to mutual embarrassment. The secret is to ask portions you want to move to stand up. THEN ASK THEM TO COME UP

FRONT. Then thank them, and tell them why you did it (you like to be close to your audience, it makes you feel better and makes you a better speaker, etc.).

Hopefully, a chairperson or M.C. will take care of all these problems and also give you a good introduction, leaving you free to concentrate on your talk.

THOSE CRITICAL FIRST TWO MINUTES

The audience is sitting there wondering "Who is this guy (or gal)?" "I certainly hope she (or he) is good." Or, despite your introduction, their thoughts may still be outside the room. They may need a short warm-up period to "erase" a previous presentation or some of the cares of the day. Put them at ease.

Recently I saw a particularly effective opening useful for foreign-born presenters who, while they speak English, do so haltingly with a heavy accent and would be more at home with their native tongue. In this case the speaker was a native of China who, when introduced, launched into a rapid-fire recitation of Chinese which certainly caught everyone's interest. After a few seconds he paused, translated his opening, and said, "Obviously it would be much easier for me to give this talk in Chinese. However, it is for your benefit that I will attempt to do it in English. Please then, excuse my accent." This opening put both the audience and the speaker immediately at ease.

Some other sample opening remarks were given in Chapter 4, and no doubt you've incorporated a variation of one of them into your talk. Above all, keep your opening brief. Then lead with your ace, the main reason you are there. Convince your listeners in that next minute and everything that follows will become a confirmation.

Whatever you do, don't give in to the old, "Let's everybody stand up and introduce ourselves" opening sometimes used as a time filler by novices with nothing better to say. For any group of over ten people, it becomes long and boring. Even with smaller groups it can make the introverts uncomfortable and/or encourage the extroverts to steal the meeting.

And, finally, *never make excuses!* I know you didn't put phrases such as "I didn't really have much time to prepare this talk," or, "I'm not much of a public speaker," in your script when you wrote it. Don't succumb to the temptation to use them now. Be positive.

How to Energize Your Audience—The AMP Formula

An ampere is a unit for measuring the strength of an electric current, and its abbreviation—AMP—provides a convenient acronym for remembering three things that can electrify or energize your audience:

- *Appearance* has a subliminal effect. It includes not only what you are wearing, but your stance (head up, shoulders erect for a confident, alert appearance) and poise (confidence and assurance). Remember, you are your most important visual.
- *Movement* can energize your audience despite the fact that they are sitting still. Don't get locked behind the lectern like a department store dummy. Move sideways, or out toward the audience, to signify a new point or to answer a question. Move over to your visuals to point out a specific item. Don't hide your hands. Use them to make some of the gestures you practiced in Chapter 7.
- *Personality* can best be shown by a slight smile. If the situation warrants a broader smile, go ahead. Smiling at an audience will make it easier for them to like you. As part of that smile, make sure you establish eye contact with your audience, showing you are interested in them as individuals.

It's amazing how much of an impression you will make on your audience in those first two minutes. I once did some consulting work for an organization interested in screening employees as potential spokespersons. The initial screening (to be followed by additional training) was based on a two-minute introduction. Hundreds of people were screened. I picked out ten evaluations that I thought might be helpful (see page 143). As you scan through them, pick out those assets you want to copy and build on, and be aware of the liabilities (set in *italics*) you want to avoid.

En Theos—"God Within"

The Greek *en theos*, meaning "god within," gives the root for the word *enthusiasm*. I like to think of it as a god-like spirit that lies within each of us, waiting to be tapped. Of course various speakers are capable of varying levels of enthusiasm, and different speaking situations call for different approaches. This is *not* to suggest that you try to imitate the announcer on television who does the "It cuts, it chops, it dices, it slices" commercial, or John Moschitta, the guy with the machine-gun mouth for Federal Express ("Pittsburgh's perfect, Peter. May I call you Pete?"). Enthusiasm is much more than talking loud and fast. However, you *should* let some of that god-like spirit within you come out in the form of movement, gestures, and vocal variety. (Some speakers even have enthusiastic eyes.) As a result, your audience will know that you are interested in what you have to say. Chances are they will be, too.

SPEAKER EVALUATIONS

Speaker	Pluses and Minuses

1. Told of personal experience. Got away from lectern. Inspirational message. No loss for words. Lots of "you's" and "your's" in talk. Could be quite good with more experience. Called others by name. *Ending was somewhat abrupt.*

2. Gestured. Message had meaning. A fun person. Handled needling well. Praised group. Good accent added interest. *Sometimes vague. Needed to be more specific.* Good closing message.

3. *Audible sigh. Parade rest position. Needs work on eye contact.* Good smile (when it's "on"). Told story from real life. Cited magazine article. Used rhetorical questions. Conversational style. Easy to listen to.

4. Historical facts interesting. Good smile. Obviously a happy person. *Used notes.* Personal glimpse showed us a very open, honest person. Likable. *Spent too much time looking down.* Otherwise at ease.

5. Got off to fast start. Winning personality. People will like her. Determination shows. Used repetition for emphasis. *Needs to avoid "rock-a-bye baby" position.* Discussed common problem shared by others. Talked directly to individuals.

6. Two favorite positions: *Hands in pocket and fig leaf.* Good appearance and voice. *Needs to slow down a little.* Mentioned others in group by name. *A little too static. Locked behind lectern.* Needs work on eye contact.

7. Good, modern appearance. Lively eyes/eyebrows. *Told good joke, but what was the point?* Expressed pride in work. *Too commercial (unnatural) at times.* Smooth transition into wrap-up.

8. *Nervous? Voice pitch changes. Shouldn't have ended with, "That's all I have to say." Needs to be more lively.* Did pose challenge for group action (i.e. "asked for the order"). In general, quality improved with time. *Maintain better level throughout. Warm up?*

9. Sounds like a believer! Proud of work. At ease. *Needs more gestures. Work on eye contact.* Well received. *Too many "ahs."* Very lively.

10. *Both hands in pockets.* Interest in family and job transfers to audience. Mellow voice. Good speaker. Has tough job. Mentioned people who inspired him. *Ran out of gas at end. Should have stopped sooner.*

HOW TO TELL IF YOU'RE LOSING THEM

I wish someone would invent a monitoring device to measure the vital signs of an audience. It would have to measure more than just breathing and heartbeat—that would only tell us if they were still alive. It would have to measure hearing, sight, attention, interest, understanding, body comfort, excitement, and a host of other functions. Such equipment would be a milestone in the development of better speakers and, possibly, better audiences.

In the meantime you will have to rely on the oral and visual feedback currently at your disposal. Orally, you can tell a lot about your listeners from the questions they ask (or the lack thereof) and the arguments they pose. Good eye contact will tell you even more. Here are some danger signals to look for:

- They start lighting up cigarettes.
- They start looking around the room or at their watches (or worse yet, shaking them).
- Nodding does not necessarily mean agreement. It may merely mean they're still listening—or worse.
- Yawns, fidgets, dozing, and loosening of ties are all sure signs to look for. When everybody reaches for the water pitcher at the same time, you're in trouble.
- Watch for that glazed look. It's called "taking an excursion" or "going down Route 350."*
- Worst of all is the door at the back of the room opening and closing as your audience trickles away.

Be at one with your audience. Stay tuned in to them with both your eyes and your ears. React. What do you do? You can't drop to your knees and pray! But you can:

- Repeat any complicated ideas, downshifting to a lower gear if they appear not to understand.
- Turn on more steam, tell a story, ask a question, stop talking, show something, give the audience something to do, talk *to* specific people. Use their name tents or badges to work in their names.
- If a sailor isn't getting the right wind, a different tack is tried. "Let me depart from this prepared address to tell you about . . ." can be magic words.

---

*The number 350 results from subtracting the rate of speech (150 words per minute maximum) from the rate at which an audience can think (500 words per minute or more). Thus, the 350 represents an excess capacity that can lead to daydreaming or other extracurricular mental activity.

- Some people in the audience bring their bodies, but leave their minds at home. Jolt them! Get them to do something—call for a show of hands. ("How many of you have actually seen a welding robot?")
- Review your main points (or preview the next ones) with a fingertip enumeration to either give them a second shot or alert them to what's coming.

If boredom is going to strike, it usually hits an audience in the second half of a presentation. Keep in mind that boredom isn't always entirely the speaker's fault. When you give your presentation, chances are you may be speaking to an audience that has had a long, tough day and is now breathing second-hand air in a smoke-filled room.

Although boredom may not be your fault, you're the one who's stuck with it. When their eyes start to droop and their stomachs start to growl—quit. Better yet, before that happens, quit while you're still ahead!

AVOIDING SIDETRACKS AND OFF RAMPS

There are other ways to lose an audience. First there are the sidetracks or tangents you may be tempted to take as you elaborate on a point in which you are particularly interested. Then there are mechanical breakdowns or other errors. And finally there's that horrible feeling of watching your audience disappear down an off ramp while you attempt to cruise merrily ahead on the main route.

Typical off ramps include such distractions and interruptions as:

- Late arrivals or early departures.
- Telephones ringing or messages brought in.
- Maintenance personnel, or gardeners at work within sight or sound of your meeting.
- Side meetings or talkers.
- And, possibly, meeting monopolizers, hecklers, or even drunks.

Never ignore an interruption. You've already lost the audience's attention. Acknowledge the interruption, then proceed.

In some cases, you can even turn an interruption into an asset. Let's suppose someone walks in late. Whatever you do, avoid the temptation to crack a joke. (They may have been in an accident, had some family problems, or been hit with some other misfortune.) Instead, show some concern and offer to quickly review the material covered so far. In addition to giving that individual some extra attention, you're providing a summary for the entire group—particularly those who may have been on an excursion. And, of course, you've smoothly handled the interruption. This technique is particularly valuable if some VIP is going to be late, since it allows you to proceed without waiting an undue amount of time.

Early leavers are a different matter. Hopefully, they will exit at the break, or sit in the back and go quietly. If they pose a distraction, some comment is in order. "Sorry you have to leave us. I'll give you a call tomorrow (or please call me)." Or, less seriously, you might say, "I didn't realize this talk was so moving"* as a good response.

Suppose the coffee arrives in the middle of your talk and it poses a distraction. Pause. Thank the person who brought it, mentioning, "It's good to see it here early." Then continue with, "We'll be taking our coffee break in just a few minutes, but first let's take a look at . . ."

Dr. Herb True, a renowned speaker who works out of South Bend, Indiana, tells of giving a seminar in a hotel and being interrupted by a maintenance man who came in carrying a stepladder in order to change a light bulb, explaining, "I get off at four, and if I don't fix this now, it won't get fixed."

True's immediate inclination was toward anger, but instead he controlled himself. Remembering some of his own advice for handling interruptions, he said, "Gee, that's great. You know, that darn flickering bulb has been bothering me all day, and it's good to see someone take such an interest in his work. As a matter of fact I'll mention this to the assistant manager on my way out tonight." (And, to himself, he added "You bet your sweet bippy I'll mention it.")

By now the maintenance man had departed, and True, gloating a little, explained to his class that he had just given us a demonstration in how to handle interruptions. But, no sooner had True finished, than the maintenance man came back in to change another light bulb. In the two years he had been working at the hotel, this was probably the first time anybody had fed his hunger for respect, recognition, and appreciation, and he wanted another "warm fuzzy."

Telephones are worse than maintenance men. Having a telephone in the room is asking for interruptions. Have it disconnected if possible. And ask that any messages be taped on the outside wall near the door unless they are absolutely urgent.

---

*You can also use this one if someone's chair tips over.

Side meetings and talkers present yet another distraction. You can afford to ignore them for a little while. Next, try silence and a stare—waiting as long as necessary. Eventually you may have to address them with one of the following:

- "It seems we're missing something. Would you care to share that with the rest of us?"
- "Roland, Jane has a good idea over here, let's give her a chance." (During questions and answers.)
- And finally, "Gentlemen (or ladies), could we have one meeting *please!*"

One of the best people at handling distractions I know of is Bill Sears, head of a management consulting firm in San Francisco. Bill is meticulous in this area, even to the point of stipulating crushed ice in the water pitchers rather than those noisy cubes. Once after listening to all his advice, a group of us attending one of his seminars conspired with the hotel staff to set him up for a series of distractions and he handled them all beautifully—the message brought into the room, the dishes crashing in the kitchen, even the vacuum cleaner next door. Only when the hotel manager walked her dog in one side of the room and out the other side did Bill catch on, pause, and shaking his head, moan, "You bastards."

Eventually you may run into a "bastard" in your audience in the form of a heckler or a drunk. Notice that by heckler I'm not referring to someone who simply has a different opinion they would like to have expressed, but to someone who threatens to take over the meeting.

Don't let them do it. Let them arrange their own meeting and gather their own audience. Give them a chance to express their views, but not to deliver a "political" tirade. During questions and answers, insist on questions, not statements. And insist on one question at a time. Open forum meetings in the civic sector frequently require patient listening to emotional arguments that sometimes border on personal abuse. Keep your cool. Don't lose control by playing the other person's game.

You are much more likely to run into meeting monopolizers than you are hecklers or drunks. Monopolizers usually tip their hands by asking more questions than the rest of the group combined. Once after I gave a report-writing training session for the Society of Technical Communications, the chairman told me, "Your seminar was great, and I particularly liked the way you handled old 'so-and-so'." "Who?" I replied. "You know," he answered, "you really put him in his place on all those 'smart' questions." Well, to tell the truth, I *didn't* know. Yes, one individual had asked a lot of questions, but I had tried to treat them as honest questions and answer them to the best of my ability. And this would still be my choice if I were to run into the same situation tomorrow.

The only exception might be if the same individual continued to ask a lot of really stupid questions. This happened to me one day in Pensacola, Florida. An individual had asked a series of pretty dumb questions, and I had handled them in a normal fashion. But it was apparent to me and the rest of the group that he just liked to hear himself talk and would engage his mouth without having his mind in gear. Obviously an advanced case of foot-in-mouth disease. Finally, I was talking about the disadvantages of read talks and said, "To borrow some terminology from the streets, a read talk is a downer. The head goes down, the eyes go down . . ." The audience was composed of young people familiar with the term "downer," but he chose to interrupt in mid-sentence with, "Wait a minute, do you expect us to give talks on street corners?"

Perhaps it was being stopped in mid-sentence that did it! While I paused to recollect my thoughts, my mind did a flashback and I said, "You know, this reminds me of my boyhood, growing up on the farm. I knew I wasn't cut out to be a farmer. Actually I wanted to be an electrical engineer, and I spent most of my time fooling around with gadgets I had invented. One was an electric flyswatter that I hooked up for my father's prize mule.

"Well, I wasn't cut out to be much of an electrical engineer either. Never could remember if it was E = IR or vice versa. As a result, I electrocuted that poor mule.

"Now my father had a terrible temper, and I was really afraid of what he would do to me when he came out to the barn and found the dead mule. I knew he'd be looking for me. Well, he discovered me cowering behind the woodshed, which shows there were a lot of things I wasn't very smart about.

"Surprisingly, instead of being enraged, he was very calm. I think my mother may have had a chance to talk to him first. He merely said, 'Son, I know you meant well, but that was a terrible thing you did to that poor mule, and *one of these days that jackass may return to haunt you.'* "

Looking up at the group, I then added, "And I think *today* is the day."

That stopped the incessant, inane questions from that individual without inhibiting questions from the rest of the group. As a matter of fact it served as an icebreaker and they got more involved. Later I apologized to the individual, and still later I asked one of the more senior speakers what she would have done. Her reply: "Next time don't apologize."

Actually, the first time I heard the jackass story it was used by a stand-up comic to quiet a drunk in the Poconos. A quicker, more effective method is to ask the inebriate to repeat the statement or question. Usually he or she will have some difficulty doing so, which may be enough in itself. If not, it will give you a little more time to think of a comeback.

Whether it's a heckler, drunk, or monopolizer, keep in mind that the audience will invariably be on your side. They're just as irritated by the irrelevant interruptions as you are.

IF DISASTER STRIKES, REACH FOR A LIFE PRESERVER

Anyone who knows the first thing about boats would never think of going out in one without a life preserver. As a speaker there are a few life preservers you need to have handy at the lectern.

The first is a glass of water. Chances are you won't have any trouble with your throat, but better to have a glass of water up there just in case. It certainly beats running down the hall gagging.

Another life preserver is a brief set of speaker's notes with the main points you plan to cover and a few pertinent statistics. A single 8½ by 11 sheet should suffice. The sample sheet on page 150 shows how one can be constructed. Notice that its division into three parts allows it to be folded easily, aiding its concealment if carried to the lectern. I use this type of life preserver on a 1¼ hour presentation entitled "You, the Talk, and the Audience," and it serves me quite well.

The beginning of this chapter talked about every speaker having butterflies in the stomach and ways to keep them under control. But suppose a few get out and fly around the room where people can see them? If this happens, you want to make sure that they are at least flying in formation.

The speaker can't paint over mistakes like an architect, or bury them like a doctor. But chances are your mistakes aren't that serious. Every speaker makes mistakes, and usually the audience doesn't notice.

If your memory runs out or you get going too fast and leave something out, forget it. Or, if it's really important, stick it back in with an "Oh, by the way . . ." or remember to cover it in your wrap-up.

What do you do if you turn a chart too early? According to Bill Sears, if you even touch the chart go ahead and turn it if at all possible. Don't call attention to mistakes by going back to correct them.

Sears also has some good advice on what to do if an annoying wrinkle begins to develop along the top of your charts as you flip them. Take a moment to straighten it out with a tug on the back of the chart, or if the wrinkle still won't come out, pull at the corners. Otherwise you will have an irritant both to yourself and the audience that will, if left uncorrected, get progressively worse with the turn of each new chart.

What if you push the slide change button too early or if you push it and nothing happens? If you are too early, try not to go back. The audience won't know there's a problem until you call their attention to it. If you pushed and nothing happened, try again (a little firmer) before you check for a malfunction. If there is a malfunction, determine whether it can be fixed quickly. If not, call for questions while someone else looks into it, or let the audience take a break while you do.

——— OPENING REMARKS ———		
(Main theme, its importance, your credentials, etc.)		
TOPIC A	TOPIC B	TOPIC C
Major Point	Similar to A	Similar to A
— Logic or Supporting Evidence		
— Supporting Evidence		
— Supporting Evidence		
— Supporting Evidence		
Major Point		
— Logic or Supporting Evidence		
— Supporting Evidence		
— Supporting Evidence		
— Supporting Evidence		
Major Point		
—		
—		
—		
—		

Single-sheet speaker's notes

If you are working with a projectionist, don't be too fast to cry wolf. If a slide comes up too early, try to move on in your narration. If one doesn't come up right away, give the projectionist a chance to catch up before you press the signal a second time. Otherwise you may wind up with two slide changes.

Don't raise hell with the projectionist or anyone else if things go wrong. Keep calm. Be a gentleman or a lady. Disasters are only disasters when the speaker lets them become so.

In 1964, when Governor James A. Rhodes of Ohio and President Lyndon Johnson attended the 160th anniversary of Ohio University, Governor Rhodes intended to say, "This venerable institution." Instead he proclaimed it, "This venereal institution."[16] Touching, very touching. If something you inadvertently say breaks up the audience, try to enjoy the laugh along with them.

PACING YOURSELF

In order to get your talk off on the right foot, start on time. If you feel you must delay, keep it under five minutes at the very most. Why punish those who are prompt in order to accommodate latecomers? If late arrivals cause a distraction, you can recapitulate as explained earlier.

The only thing more important than starting on time is finishing on time. Have an associate in the back of the room signal the time remaining. Finish a few minutes early and leave your audience wanting more. I'm convinced that there is a special corner in hell where long-winded speakers are forced to endure an eternity of public television membership drives. The mere thought of it should help you keep your talks short.

If you don't enforce self-discipline regarding time, the audience will by tuning you out. And remember that time is more critical for a VIP audience. Reestablish how much time is available before you start, and be ready to readjust. If you've grabbed their interest, they'll keep it going beyond the "official" time with their questions. *Don't rush them at this stage.* The end of their questions will tell you when to say thanks.

What if you are part of an agenda, and one or more previous speakers have run over, and the chairperson has allowed them to use up a major portion of your time, perhaps backing you up against lunch or the end of the day? Since the moderator didn't take charge earlier, you must do so now. One speaker I know faced this problem by starting his talk with, "And in conclusion . . ." and then gave his summary. A better approach would be to negotiate a new contract, reaching an agreement with your audience before you start. Basically, they have two choices:

1. You will give your talk, making up whatever time possible, but recognizing the schedule will run at least ____ minutes over.
2. Recognizing that their cumulative experience is no doubt greater than yours, you can offer an open discussion of their interests, problems, or suggestions, with you serving as moderator and "tailgating" with (inserting) portions of your prepared talk where appropriate. Promise to end on schedule.

Their politeness may predispose them in favor of the first alternative, but if you get a chance, sway them toward the second. You may not get an opportunity to show all your visuals or make all your points, but synergism may ensue, making the end result much more effective. You may even become a hero!

THAT BIG FINISH

Chapter 4 covered interesting endings for your presentation, and presented the speaker who, with a tone of relief, suddenly says, "Thank you," and abruptly sits down. Remember, there's nothing wrong with thanking your audience, but it ought to be a little more elaborate. And the fact that you've come to the end should not be a surprise reminiscent of the old camping song, "I guess you think this is the end. Well, it is."

The closing is really the time for the big finish. Step forward to meet the audience and launch your summary or wrap-up. "Now that I have finished presenting my case, let me stress one fact . . ." Then restate your chief benefit. Are you sure they know what you want them to do? Do they know why action is important now instead of later? Did you "Ask for the order?" After the question-and-answer session you might acknowledge their comments warmly. Use, "I appreciate your sharing your ideas with me . . ."

STANDING OVATIONS ARE SOMETIMES EASY TO GET

I hope the end of your talk is greeted with applause, and that the applause is based on content, not merely on the fact that it's concluded. If your presentation was really outstanding you may even get a standing ovation. (Spontaneous standing ovations are rare, but you can usually get one for someone else or a committee fairly easily by subtly suggesting it—particularly if the audience is large and has been sitting for a long time. Try it.)

Maybe you will merely get a thank you or a nod of the head. Whatever. Giving a good presentation is its own reward, knowing that you have sold yourself and your ideas.

CHAPTER TEN

Questions and Answers: The Speaker's Dessert

"QUESTIONS AND ANSWERS are the speaker's dessert?" you ask. Well, there's more to that analogy than just the fact that questions and answers follow the main course. Like dessert, questions and answers add something extra, something special that can be sweet and satisfying, something to look forward to. Indeed, in many cases, the question-and-answer session can be more important than the presentation itself.

However, instead of looking forward to questions and answers, some speakers dread the session. They feel it will wreck their presentation. Good speakers should look on questions as an opportunity. They should cast aside the W-R-E-C-K and concentrate on the R-E-C—seizing an opportunity to Repeat, Emphasize, and Clarify.

Certainly, having an audience ask questions does pose a degree of risk. Just as soldiers are sometimes killed in battle after an armistice has been signed, so speakers can be hit by a "stray bullet" after their ending. But the benefits of questions and answers far outweigh the risks. Don't pass up this opportunity to start a dialogue, do additional tailoring, and provide more details that your audience wants to know.

"ARE THERE ANY QUESTIONS?"

All of us have heard speakers finish a talk by asking this question. Frequently it's followed by a microsecond pause before the speaker says "Thank you," and sits down. What the speaker is really saying, internally, is, "Thank God it's over!"

What a missed opportunity! Don't let it ever happen to you. Dialogue is what presentations are all about; it's what separates them from reports and proposals or formal speeches. The question-and-answer session provides feedback on your ideas. Despite any misgivings you may have, you *want* questions. Here are some ways to make sure you get them:

- As part of your introduction, the chairperson should announce that questions will be welcome. And, if the chairperson forgets, you should make the announcement. You might even elaborate a little to drive the point home. Tell them you're looking forward to the Q & A portion. Ask them to jot down any particular items they would like to discuss further.

- At the conclusion of your talk, the chairperson can provide a smooth transition between the main body and the Q & A portion by thanking you and then asking for questions. If there isn't a chairperson or M.C., you should thank the audience, pause, and then ask for questions. In either case it usually helps to alert the audience to how much time is remaining. ("I see that we have ten minutes remaining. Are there any questions?")

- Be prepared to wait for that first question. Just because it doesn't pop up immediately doesn't mean it isn't out there. Perhaps someone in the audience is thinking about how to phrase the question. Most speakers are uncomfortable with silence at this stage, but you can let that silence work on the audience instead of on you. Ten seconds at this point may seem like an eternity. Put it to good use. Use it to rest.

- If no questions are forthcoming, you have a decision to make. Turn them loose or keep trying? Ask yourself, "Is there more to be gained?" If the answer is "yes," a little prodding may be in order. One technique is to state, "Well, if no one wants to ask the *first* question, would someone like to ask the *second*?" This usually will break the ice. Another technique is to turn the tables on them, "Well, if you don't have any questions for me, I have a few for you. Did you all understand (or agree with) the portion of my talk dealing with . . ."

- Many times, getting questions is like getting olives out of a jar—after the first one, the rest come easily. You can get the questioning started by planting one in advance with someone you know in the audience. Or, if this seems somewhat underhanded, merely get someone to promise they will ask a question of their own choosing. Tell them how important the Q & A portion is, and ask them to help get things started if need be, or to hold their question until a lull in the Q & A and ask it then to keep things going.

WHY AUDIENCES ASK QUESTIONS

A few of the many reasons audiences ask questions are: for attention, to test you, to help you (or sometimes to hurt you), to seek help, to show how knowledgeable they are, to make their own points with preambles to their questions, to lay the groundwork for a second question, for approval, and to just hear themselves talk. But usually questions are asked to gain information. Whatever their reasons, it's not the rationale behind the question, but how you handle it that's important.

HANDLING QUESTIONS

After you have had a chance to study the following suggestions on how to handle questions, you'll feel a lot more comfortable with the Q & A session. Further reinforcement will occur each time you practice—so get started.

Receive All Questions Cordially

How you handle questions is most important. Never react as though someone is trying to put you on the spot. Don't be defensive. Don't assume that the questioner is your adversary. Instead, assume that the question is being asked because you are the expert and the audience is seeking your help. Respond with introductory phrases such as: "I'm glad you asked . . ."; "That's a good question . . ."; or, "Many people are concerned about that . . ."

Don't show impatience with a question you've already covered in the main body of your talk. The fact that it was missed earlier may be as much your fault as theirs. Instead, use the question as an opportunity to repeat, emphasize, and clarify. Calling attention to the fact that they "obviously weren't listening" won't win you any Mr. Nice Guy awards with any of the members of the audience.

Be Sure You Listen Carefully

Listen actively. Be alert and attentive. Listen for tone of voice, emphasis, and inflections—but above all, listen for content.

Make sure you understand the question. Ask for clarification if necessary, or clarify it yourself by restating it for the benefit of those in the audience who may not have heard it. Lack of attention or the size of the room may cause half your audience to miss the question, particularly if the questioner is in the front half of the room with his or her back to most of the audience. Restating a question will also give you an opportunity to modify any "inflammatory" words in the original. Above all, restating or asking for clarification gives you time to think about your answer.

Don't Shoot from the Lip

Grammar school has left all of us with a Pavlovian passion to answer questions as quickly as possible to show how smart we are and gain the teacher's approval. Speakers suffer from this same passion, and sometimes will be so quick that they supply the right answer, but to the wrong question. In other words, the answer is on the way before the question has been heard (or at least understood). Or, they find themselves trapped by comments they may regret later. The result is called foot-in-mouth disease, a result of putting your mouth in motion before your brain is in gear.

So try to avoid instantaneous answers. Audiences can be irritated by smugness or the rehearsed "party line." A very slight pause—counting slowly to three—is enough. In that time you can decide:

- Why was the question asked?
- How does this fit my objectives?
- How can I condense my answer?

Answer with a KISS

The KISS formula—Keep It Short and Simple—also applies to your answers to questions. We've all heard answers that were so long we forgot what the question was. There's no need to make another speech. During Q & A, audiences tend to be dubious of any high-blown language or catch phrases.

Keep your answers brief (but not just "yes" or "no," which would stifle dialogue.) Think of a short, to-the-point answer, perhaps supported by a reason or example.

Make your point immediately. Think in terms of a newspaper article where the headline tells the story, followed by more detail. How much detail will depend on the depth of interest (and expertise) of the audience and any time constraints you may be facing. Thirty seconds should be enough.

You might even extend the KISS formula to KISSS, with the third s standing for singular. Keep it short, simple, and singular. Avoid multiple-part answers that become confusing.

However, you should have additional supporting material available for questioners who request or demand it. This can be in the form of a single sheet or even a three-ring binder containing in-depth statistics you would not be expected to remember. Or, it can be in the form of additional slides or viewgraphs you "hadn't planned to use but brought along anyway because they were available." In either case you will have to be sufficiently familiar with the material to find it quickly and discuss it intelligently.

Case histories, statistics, statements by experts, and first-hand observations can all come in handy.

Let's suppose you represent the National Park Service, which has decided to reduce the thirty-six-hole golf courses at Haines Point in Washington, D.C. to a twenty-seven-hole layout.* The forty-five acres gained will be used to eliminate traffic problems, and to add 150 parking spaces, six ball diamonds, and additional picnic areas. Sounds well and good, but you run into opposition from a group of retired and elderly golfers who favor the nine holes being converted because the shorter fairways suit their game.

Thus, the East Potomac Golf Association is formed, letters are written, personal appeals are made to congressmen, petitions are circulated, and strong criticism is leveled at the Park Service. You have the job of answering the opposition's questions at public meetings and in the media.

Well, working the foregoing statistics into your answers would help. And having some more ammunition available would certainly come in handy. For example, suppose surveys showed golfers make up only sixteen percent of the people using the park, but the thirty-six holes occupy sixty-five percent of the land.

As to the particular nine holes selected for conversion, these nine offer an opportunity to construct a new road that would connect with existing roads and relieve congestion.

Then you could add that the decision was not made lightly. Over

*Based on an actual situation as reported by Joe Pichirallo in the Washington Post.

two-and-one-half years were spent studying alternatives, city and federal planners were consulted, and public hearings held.

Finally you might add that the Park Service will try to meet the needs of the senior golfers by realigning the fairways on one of the three remaining courses.

As a result of having done your homework, you and the Park Service come away looking a little bit better in the eyes of the general public.

If You Don't Know, Say So

No one likes to be hit with a question to which they don't know the answer. We don't like to admit that we just don't know. But, the consequences of bluffing, guessing, or faking an answer are much worse.

I was once in a meeting where the speaker was queried concerning the costs associated with a certain approach. He sighed and disdainfully replied "peanuts." This was quickly met by a second question, "And would you mind telling us exactly what peanuts are selling for this year?" And so, the speaker finally admitted he didn't know—in this case to his plant manager.

Wouldn't it have been much better to say, "I don't know the cost of that particular item, but I'll have it for you before you leave today"? In this case you've demonstrated candor, indicated that you know where to find the answer, and established a time limit for responding.

Sometimes you can throw a question back at the audience, asking their opinions. After all, the sum of their collective expertise may well outweigh yours. This increases dialogue and may flatter the audience. I've used this technique frequently on the seminar circuit. Many times the answer I got from the group in Detroit made me look like a whiz the next week in Des Moines.

If you've done a thorough job on your homework, you'll be able to answer ninety percent of the questions. Rehearsing potential questions may raise that percentage even higher.

Rehearse the Questions and Answers

At first, the thought of rehearsing potential questions and answers may strike you as ridiculous, abhorrent, or both. But it can make a lot of sense. The Q & A session can often be more important than the presentation itself. In these cases, rehearsing questions and answers not only makes sense, it would be stupid not to. Indeed, I have seen rehearsals where more time was spent on questions and answers than on anything else. Most organizations, however, sadly neglect this area.

Why rehearse the answers? So that you can deliver them with machine-gun rapidity? Of course not. Instead, you are preparing your ammunition. Finding those areas where more backup data will be required. Anticipating objections.

How many times have you found yourself thinking, "Gee, I should (or shouldn't) have said . . . " That's what such a rehearsal will provide, an opportunity to take a second look at your answers. And, if you are taking that second look via video tape, here are some things to look and listen for.

Watch Out for Eye Contact

Look directly at the individual asking the question as long as she or he is talking. You want your entire attention focused on the person talking and what is being said, and you want the questioner to know it. During the initial phase of your answer, maintain that eye contact. But as you get into more detail, feel free to break that contact and shift to others. (This will help avoid a series of followup questions resulting in the possibility of a dialogue between just the two of you.) Always return to the individual who asked the question initially. Does the questioner look satisfied, puzzled, or angry? If appropriate, rephrase your answer or ask if you answered the right question.

Stock Phrases Worth Studying

If you're using a video tape to record your practice Q & A session, listen to the tone of your answers. Did you choose your words carefully? Did you sound credible? Pompous? Antagonistic? Hurt? Here are some examples of good approaches:

- "I'm sorry I missed getting the point across. I should have stated that more clearly." (Instead of, "You missed my point.")
- "Your point is well taken."
- "Let me clarify that a bit." (Instead of, "You don't understand.")
- "I didn't mean to slight that."
- "Am I glad you asked that question."

- "Bear with me one more second."
- "If this were a true/false test, the answer would be easy. But it's going to take more than that."
- "Did I answer the right question?"

It's tough to agree, yet disagree. If a questioner asks, "Wouldn't it be possible to . . .?" try, "Well, it would if you include . . ., however . . .," instead of, "Naw, that won't work!" Be careful of "Do you understand (or follow) me?" and "OK?" and "You know?" Many people will suspect a subliminal "stupid" implied therein.

Body Language

The importance of appropriate body language—particularly the position of your arms—is as great as it was at the start of your presentation. Various books on body language state that crossed arms are a sign of being closed-minded or of rejection. Do you have your arms crossed as you answer questions? You may merely be cold or have them crossed for personal comfort. But those in the audience who have read about body language—and even those who haven't—may reach other conclusions.

Do you find your head dropping down as you think, or find yourself shifting from foot to foot? The likely impression there is uncertainty and shiftiness. If necessary, rest your chin on one hand, with the other across your chest. The impression now changes to one of contemplation.

These tips all deal with routine questions. Most will fall in this category, and you shouldn't have too much trouble handling them. But when you want questions to be asked is another problem you'll have to face.

WHEN DO YOU WANT QUESTIONS?

Of course, you always want questions. But you have some degree of control over whether they will be asked during your presentation or saved until the end. The choice depends on a number of factors. Your own style and what you are most comfortable with will help you decide. The type of audience will play a role. With extremely busy executives, a question you can't answer in the middle of your presentation (e.g., "How much will this cost?" or "Has it been budgeted?") could effectively end the presentation right there. The type of visuals used will also have an effect. (For example, a slide presentation with its darkened room discourages questions.) So will your time limitations and subject matter. If you are developing an extremely complex idea that requires continuity, you may not want questions during your presentation. Otherwise you probably will, because questions provide an opportunity to establish rapport and find out if you are reaching the group.

Be sure your audience knows at the outset whether you want them to ask questions during your talk or to hold them for the end. And if you are serving on a panel, the audience should know whether questions will be accepted after each speaker or should be held until everyone is finished.

Questions during the Presentation

Generally, this is the better approach, particularly with a small audience. It gets the audience involved, gives you feedback, and maintains the timeliness of both question and answer.

Just as a radar sends out a pulse and listens for a return, be sure that you go into the "receive" mode occasionally. Don't always be transmitting. Be alert for questions. Nothing is more embarrassing than having a question asked, missing it, and keeping right on talking. Better eye contact and pauses will prevent this from happening.

If you entertain questions during your presentation you will occasionally run up against one that is premature; that is, one that involves a topic you will be explaining in a few more minutes and the answer should be forthcoming. Politely table these and thank the questioners. Congratulate them for mentally moving faster than your dialogue. Tell them they are about three slides (or whatever) in front of you and you'd like to defer the question until you reach that point. Then, when you do, make sure their questions are answered.

Questions after the Presentation

Although answering questions after your talk can make a tidier presentation, it has some drawbacks. The chief one is that this portion of time is very important to you and you want to end on a high note. Leaving it to questions and answers could result in your ending on a bad question, a bad answer, or both. Instead, you want a big finish. To accomplish this you may want to reserve time for a summary after the questions to make sure you don't end on a downer.

RECOGNIZING WHEN YOU ARE BEING PUT ON THE SPOT

Sometimes you may face hostile audiences, particularly if you work in the public arena. Watch out for questions that are prefaced by, "With all due respect . . ." and for the questioner who faces the audience to ask a question. That's usually tantamount to, "Let's get this guy (or gal)!"

Types of Loaded Questions

Chances are that you'll never be put on the spot by being asked the old, "When Did You Stop Beating Your Wife?" question. But there are a number of equally perplexing questions that can catch you off guard if you are unaware of the techniques behind them. These loaded questions have become a favorite tactic of radical groups and some members of the press. As a result, a number of consulting firms offer training programs designed to teach CEO's, politicians, and other leaders how to handle them. One of the better firms in this field is Jack Hilton, Incorporated. Here is a summary of their advice on various types of loaded questions and how to handle them.[17]

The A or B Dilemma is a no-win situation. The questioner asks, "I find it outrageous that your organization has . . . Is that due to greed or ineptness?" Or the question is "Is your company more interested in profits or the public?" or, "Which is nuttier to deal with, Country X or Country Y?" When you find yourself faced with this type of dilemma, don't opt for the lesser of two evils. The world isn't all black and white. Who says the answer has to be A or B? It can be C or D or E. You should answer the three questions posed above as follows: 1) "Well, of course it's neither . . ." 2) "Obviously we are interested in both . . ." 3) "Neither, and I think that's a poor choice of words . . ."

The Irrelevant Question can be a trap set by someone trying to stir up controversy. Let's suppose you are "Mr. Wonderful" representing the Boy Scouts of America and a questioner asks you how you feel about marijuana. Don't react to the stimulus by saying, "Well, in my own personal opinion . . ." This won't work because you are a spokesperson for the Boy Scouts and your personal opinion is irrelevant. Your answer should be "The Boy Scouts of America has no written position on marijuana, but we encourage boys to obey the laws; *all* the laws." Thus you have taken the initiative and are free to go on to make whatever point you wish.

The Absent Party Question puts you in the role of answering for someone else. Examples might include: "Do you think the President's stand on _____ was politically motivated?" or, "Why are people like Senator Mugwump out to get you?" Here your answers would be, "I can't speculate on his motives," or, "I really can't guess at that, your guess is as good as mine," or, "Why don't you ask him?" And, if appropriate, you might add, "I can, however, tell you what I would have done (or what I think he should have done) . . . ," thus seizing the initiative.

The Inconsistency Trap involves being reminded of how you voted the last time, or your role in establishing a previous policy. Don't steadfastly defend old outmoded policies. Only fools never change.

The Hypothetical Question usually involves a "what if." Indeed, it may include three or four "what ifs." Your best bet is probably to reply, "There are so many 'what ifs' (or, There is such a big 'what if') in that question that I think it's entirely too speculative for me to try to answer." If you elect to respond at all, feel free to put your own conditions into the record, and they can be equally "iffy." In fact, you may want to highlight the remoteness of the possibility by accentuating the if. "Well, *if* such and such were to happen, and then *if* . . ., we might have . . ., but only *if* . . ., and finally *if* . . ., so you see, *if* . . ." Or, once again, you have a chance to turn the tables with, "I think that your question assumes a situation that . . . But let's consider . . ." Again, take the initiative.

The Loaded Preface isn't a question, it's a setup or thinly veiled attack. In this situation the questioner starts with an inflammatory comment such as "Given the deservedly low regard for . . ." or, "Since you big manufacturers get together to set your prices . . ." or, "Do you mean to tell me that your agency, which has raped our environment, also . . ." and then goes on (perhaps at length) to ask an unrelated question or maybe even couples the loaded preface with an A or B dilemma. The tendency is to ignore the emotional preface or gloss over it in order to get to what you perceive as the real question. Don't do it. Since the preface has set the tone for the audience, you have to challenge it. Try, "I'd be very pleased to answer your question, but first I'd like to address your allegation." Or, "If you're going to include a speech in your question, I'm going to include a speech in my answer. First . . ." Having taken care of the loaded preface, you can then go on to the rest of the question. (But try to do this without stooping to the gutter tactics of the questioner or you may lose your audience.)

All of these loaded questions present you with an opportunity to take the initiative and continue to score points of your own. And here's how Jack Hilton recommends doing it.

Going from Defense to Offense

In handling tough questions, you want to be as positive as possible, switching the flow from the negative question to a positive answer. The technique for doing this is called bridging. Bridging consists of using transitional statements that take you from where you are to where you want to be:

- "Obviously, we have a difference of opinion, but let's not waste time arguing on that. What's more important is . . ."
- "I can understand where you might have gotten that impression, but I couldn't disagree more. Let me point out that . . ."
- "Quite the contrary. Perhaps you're not aware of . . ."

Then try to follow these with three or more positive points you can work into your answer. Go for the knockout! To do this you must be ready with objectives of your own. You have to have more than just your speech in your pocket. And that's where rehearsals or courses like Jack Hilton's come in handy.

Other Ways to Defuse Nasty Questions

In addition to bridging, there are other ways to defuse nasty questions. Watch out for labels (high impact words) in the question, like: failure, overrun, poisons, delays, swindle, slippage, pain, price-fixing, pollution—particularly any words that might be associated with a civil or criminal offense. Then restate the question for the audience without the zingers, and follow up with a positive reply.

You can also question the questioner. If you don't know why a question was asked or you think it may be a trap, ask for clarification. This will give you time to think and make it obvious to the audience what the questioner is doing.

Sometimes humor can be effective in these situations if the audience is in the right mood. If you are talking to a group that disagrees with you, but is not angry or openly hostile, you might try, "I feel about as welcome as a leper at a skin lotion convention." Or in response to a tough question, "When *he* tells you to go to hell, you're anxious to get started." Or, "I feel like a human target for a nearsighted knifethrower." Or, "I didn't come here to cuss, I came to discuss."

Above All, Stay in Control

Very few presenters can win their case by losing their cool. Be patient and kind. Agree with questioners—up to a point. If you must attack, attack the idea and not the questioner. "OK, so you're opposed to nuclear energy. Let me tell you a few things I'm opposed to—strip mining, air pollution, inflation caused by high prices for foreign oil, oil spills, etc."

Those of you familiar with Transactional Analysis will do well to keep the principles of the Parent-Child-Adult process in mind. A petulant, childish question can lead to a scolding, parental answer and vice versa. Try to keep the dialogue on a calm adult-to-adult level—or at least your side of it.

The table on page 167 lists strategies suggested by Reddy Communications and the RCI Consulting Group for handling adversary confrontation.

HANDLING THE LONG-WINDED QUESTION

Often such questions come in multiple parts, and many good speakers jot down brief notes to make sure they don't miss anything. Indeed, the audience may have forgotten parts of the question. So it might be helpful to restate the main parts with, "Let me see if I can summarize that a bit."

If the questioner is really rambling, try for a graceful cutoff. (The audience will most likely be with you.) Give the questioner a chance to run out of breath, and when there's a pause, summarize for them. Anticipate the ending, supply an answer, and move on. After a particularly long, involved, multi-faceted question, you might try, "Was there anything else?"

If the question is tangential or the answer is extremely involved, you might say, "That's a good question, but I wonder if the entire audience is sufficiently interested to warrant discussing it now. I'll be around later so that the two of us and anyone else who's interested can get into it. Are there any more questions on . . .?"

NONQUESTIONS

Sometimes you will be faced with statements disguised as questions. "Do you think these factory workers really want early retirement?" is a clue that you are about to hear what the questioner

ETHICAL STRATEGIES
FOR ADVERSARY CONFRONTATION

I.   Be Audience Centered

It is highly unlikely that you can convert your opponent, so your information and arguments should be developed with the audience in mind.

A.   *Analyze your audience*—direct arguments to their attitudes and interest. Don't dwell on minor technical details.

B.   *Stay within the audience's frame of reference*—simplify the language. Don't assume technical "know how."

C.   *Avoid "fighting" with your opponent*—getting into "one-on-one" verbal battles only creates a competitive, win/lose situation.

II.   Advance Your Position

It is imperative that you counter questions raised by your opponents about the points you advocate. There are a variety of techniques for countering an opponent's attack, such as:

A.   *Disassociate*—separate any negative comparisons between your company and other companies, events, or organizations, that are not relevant.

B.   *Give to get*—acknowledge minor problems to win major points.

C.   *Selective response*—when an adversary raises multiple issues select the one with which you feel most confident and respond to it.

D.   *Buying time*—ask questions or request further clarification to give yourself time to think.

III.   Refute Your Opponent's Position

Invalid arguments or assertions by your opponents must not go unchallenged. Such fallacies can be exposed with techniques like:

A.   *Hyperbole*—exaggeration for effect.

B.   *Flat denial*—deny inaccurate statements. (This is a good technique for "getting the floor.")

C.   *Directive questions and statements*—leading questions or statements in order to guide the discussion into your strong suits and your adversary's weak suits.

D.   *Play it out*—show the consequences if your adversary's position is accepted by extending it or creating a scenario.

IV.   Control the Time

Your goal should be to control 60 to 70 percent of the time in discussion to allow your arguments enough development. Time control is aimed not at simply "holding the floor," but also to insure enough time to effectively state your case.

A.   *Interrupt*—closed-end question or statement to gain the floor.

B.   *Tag team*—maintain control by turning the discussion over to your teammate so that he may add to it or provide further development.

C.   *Issues list*—have a list of key issues prepared for use during lulls in the discussion.

thinks. Perhaps the questioner is making a "political" statement or merely wants to show how smart he or she is. That's OK. Accept such questions. You might even ask such questioners for more detail or their own views. Then amplify or refute what has been said with points of your own.

QUESTIONS YOU DON'T HAVE TO ANSWER

Some questions are clearly out of place, but come up as a result of thoughtlessness or an attempt to embarrass the speaker. For example, unless your salary is a matter of public record, it's nobody's business but your own. You can feel free to dismiss such questions with "I think that's a rather personal question and irrelevant to the subject under discussion. Could we have another question please?"

Don't be trapped into giving an "authoritative" answer to a question dealing with something outside your responsibility or competence. You need only say, "I'm sorry I can't answer that, the question is outside my area."

There are many other reasons why you would elect not to answer a particular question. For example, the matter may be in litigation. Try to give your audience an idea why you choose not to answer—particularly if that audience includes members of the press.

AND IF THE PRESS IS PRESENT

Years ago, there must have been a movie where the star rushed through a crowd of reporters saying, "No comment. No comment." Obviously the phrase made such an impression it's still being used today, even though in today's world, "No comment" often translates into *guilty as charged.*

Instead of saying "No comment," tell why you can't answer:

- It's in litigation.
- It's being studied and the report is due on_____.
- It's outside your area of expertise.
- You simply don't know.

Keep in mind that news is a business. Therefore it involves competition. Sometimes this results in a touch of sensationalism, especially where sensitive issues are involved.

Listen *carefully* to questions from the press. Many times their questions won't appear in the printed or broadcast version, only your answer will. So, if there is a "bad" choice of words in the question, don't repeat it in the answer. Remember that the *real* audience is not the reporter, but is all those people out there. So keep your objectives in mind. Also, keep in mind that newspeople are always newspeople. That includes at the club, on an airplane, and *after* they say, "Hey, that was a great interview." Finally, remember that in order for something to be "off the record" or for "deep background purposes," you will have to make it clear *before* you make the statement.

Remembering all this while a microphone is thrust in your face can be quite a challenge. But perhaps these tips will help you tap dance through any media minefields you might encounter. Hopefully you will never face this type of grilling. Instead, you may be actively seeking media coverage to publicize your talk. Providing it's on a newsworthy subject, you may very well be able to get some press and possibly local TV coverage as well. Here's how:

- About two weeks before the talk, send a summary to news outlets. Be sure to include a "hook" that will get them (and their audiences) interested.
- Two days before, follow up with a phone contact.
- If anyone expresses interest but can't make it, try to arrange a separate interview—perhaps at breakfast or lunch.
- Print copies of your talk as a handout or a mailer.
- If your organization has a public relations department, ask their help.

With a little luck you may be able to multiply your exposure a thousand-fold or more. Good luck!

Notes

1. Reprinted with permission from *Successful Meetings* magazine. Copyright © 1978, Bill Communications, Inc.

2. William S. Tacey, *Business and Professional Speaking*, second ed. (Dubuque: William C. Brown Co., 1975), p. 102.

3. George Plimpton, "How to Make a Speech," *Power of the Printed Word Series*, International Paper Co.

4. J. Lewis Powell, *Executive Speaking—An Acquired Skill*, revised ed. (Washington, D.C.: The Bureau of National Affairs, Inc., 1980), p. 28.

5. Abridged excerpt from Chapter 17 "To Be Exact" in *How to Write, Speak, and Think More Effectively* by Rudolf Flesch. Copyright © 1946, 1949, 1951, 1958, 1960 by Rudolf Flesch. Reprinted by permission of Harper & Row, Publishers, Inc.

6. Bob Bly, "Plotting Your Course—Storyboarding Your Slide Presentations," *Audio Visual Directions*, October/November, 1981.

7. Courtesy of Dale Carnegie and Associates, Inc.

8. Powell, op. cit., p. 58.

9. Reprinted with permission of Dr. Jerry Tarver, from "Speechwriter's Letter."

10. From *In Search of Excellence: Lessons from America's Best-Run Companies* by Thomas J. Peters and Robert H. Waterman, Jr., p. xviii. Copyright © 1982 by Thomas J. Peters and Robert Waterman, Jr. Reprinted by permission of Harper & Row, Publishers, Inc.

11. Russ Johnston, *The Marplex Digest*, April, 1983.

12. Anthony Jay, *The New Oratory* (New York: American Management Association, Inc., 1971), p. 78. Printed by kind permission of Curtis Brown on behalf of Anthony Jay © 1970.

13. Ibid., p. 79.

14. Specified excerpt (p. xx) from *In Search of Excellence: Lessons from America's Best-Run Companies* by Thomas J. Peters and Robert H. Waterman, Jr. Copyright © 1982 by Thomas J. Peters and Robert Waterman, Jr. Reprinted by permission of Harper & Row, Publishers, Inc.

15. Eve Zibart, "Psyching Up; Contortions, Potions and Meditations—How the Stars Get Ready for the Show," *The Washington Post,* August 5, 1979.

16. Foster & Green, Inc. Newsletter, December, 1982.

17. Used with permission. Copyright © 1980, Jack Hilton.

Resources

The following is a list of references and resources cited throughout this book. (Copyrighted material used with permission.)

Books

Flesch, Rudolf. *How to Write, Speak, and Think More Effectively*. New York: Harper & Row, 1960; New American Library, Signet Books, 1964 (T2346). *Page 20*.

Guth, Chester K. and Stanley S. Shaw. *How to Put on Dynamic Meetings*. Reston, VA: Reston Publishing, 1980. (Available from School Annual Publishing Co., Coshocton, OH 43812.) *Page 77*.

Jay, Anthony. *The New Oratory*. New York: American Management Association, Inc., 1971. *Pages 80 and 81*.

Kemp, Jerrold E. *Planning and Producing Audiovisual Materials*. New York: Thomas Y. Crowell, 1975. *Page 77*.

Molloy, John T. *Dress for Success*. New York: Peter H. Wyden, 1975.

———. *The Woman's Dress for Success Book*. New York: Follett, 1977. *Page 108*.

Peters, Thomas J. and Robert H. Waterman, Jr. *In Search of Excellence—Lessons from America's Best-Run Companies*. New York: Harper & Row, 1982. *Pages 77 and 82*.

Powell, J. Lewis. *Executive Speaking—An Acquired Skill*, revised edition. Washington, D.C.: The Bureau of National Affairs, Inc., 1980. *Pages 19 and 37*.

Tacey, William S. *Business and Professional Speaking*, second edition. Dubuque: William C. Brown Co., 1975. *Page 11*.

---

*Pages cited are those in this book.

Articles

Bly, Bob. "Plotting Your Course—Storyboarding Your Slide Presentations." *Audio Visual Directions*, October/November, 1981. *Page 28.*

Bombeck, Erma. "Anxiety Over Speaking." *The Evening Capital*, July 11, 1983. *Page 2.*

Finkel, Coleman. "Meeting Clinic." *Successful Meetings*, January, 1978. (Bill Communications, Inc.) *Page 6.*

Foster & Green, Inc. Newsletter, 16 E. Chase St., Baltimore, MD 21202, December, 1982. *Page 151.*

The Marplex Digest, Marplex, Inc., Chagrin Falls, OH 44022, April, 1983. *Page 79.*

Plimpton, George. "How to Make A Speech." *Power of the Printed Word Series*, International Paper Co., Box 954, Madison Square Station, New York, NY 10010. *Page 17.*

Tarver, Dr. Jerry. "Speechwriter's Letter." Box 444, The University of Richmond, Richmond, VA 23173. *Page 48.*

Zibart, Eve. "Psyching Up; Contortions, Potions and Meditations—How the Stars Get Ready for the Show." *The Washington Post*, August 5, 1979. *Page 137.*

Consulting Organizations

Jack Hilton, Inc., 60 E. 42nd St., New York, NY 10165. *Page 163.*

National Conference Centers, Coleman Finkel, President, East Windsor, NJ 08520. *Page 6.*

Organizational Renewal, Inc., Dr. Gordon Lippitt, 5605 Lamar Rd., Bethesda, MD 20816. *Page 102.*

Reddy Communications, Inc. and the RCI Consulting Group, 537 Steamboat Rd., P.O. Box 1310, Greenwich, CT 06830. *Page 167.*

W.R. Sears & Co., Management Consultants, Bill Sears, President, 3187 Greenoak Ct., San Mateo, CA 94403. *Pages 147 and 150.*

Team International, Inc., Dr. Herb True, 1717 E. Colfax, South Bend, IN 46617. *Page 146.*

A-V Suppliers

Audio Visual Division/3M, 3M Center, St. Paul, MN 55144. The leading marketer of overhead projectors and transparency film. Lettering Systems. Overhead supplies. Screens. Presentation furniture. *Pages 74 and 110.*

Cinegraph Slides, Inc., 11642 Knott Ave., Bldg. #12, Garden Grove, CA 92641. Custom-made original slides for business presentations. The customer writes copy, they do everything else. Catalog available. *Pages 74 and 76.*

Dynamic Graphics, Inc., 6000 N. Forest Park Dr., Peoria, IL 61614-3592. Publishes camera-ready artwork of exceptional quality, including: the Clipper Creative Art Service; Print Media Service; specially themed art packages. *Page 74.*

Eastman Kodak Co., Dept. 454, 343 State St., Rochester, NY 14651. Film and Projectors. Publishes numerous how-to booklets. *Page 76.*

Genigraphics Corp., Box 591, Liverpool, NY 13088. Computer graphics. *Page 76.*

Oravisual Co., Inc., Box 11150, St. Petersburg, FL 33733. Meeting equipment and training aids. Portable and wall-mounted easels. Lecterns. Sound system accessories. *Page 74.*

Schwan-STABILO USA, Inc., P.O. Box 2193, 435 Dividend Drive, Peachtree City, GA 30269. Overhead projection kits. *Page 75.*

Scott Graphics Inc./Scott Paper, Holyoke, MA 01040. Overhead supplies. *Page 75.*

Visual Horizons, "The Audio Visual Department Store," 180 Metro Park, Rochester, NY 14618. Stock and custom slides. Slide mounts, slide files, and light tables. Slide duplicating. Slides made from your PC and modem. Overhead supplies. A-V furniture. *Page 76.*

Xerox Reproduction Centers, Xerox Square 862, Rochester, NY 14644. *Page 76.*

Other

Dale Carnegie and Associates, Inc., 1475 Franklin Ave., Garden City, NY 11530. *Pages 83 and 104.*

SALLY FORTH by Greg Howard © 1983 Field Enterprises, Inc. Courtesy of Field Newspaper Syndicate. *Page 2.*

"Orben's Current Comedy," The Comedy Center, 700 Orange St., Wilmington, DE 19801. *Page 37.*

Toastmasters' International, 2200 N. Grand Ave., P.O. Box 10400, Santa Ana, CA 92711.

Suggested Reading

Bland, Michael. *The Executive's Guide to TV and Radio Appearances.* New York: Van Nostrand Reinhold, 1980.

Braude, Jacob M. *Braude's Treasury of Wit and Humor.* Englewood Cliffs, NJ: Prentice-Hall, 1964.

————. *Speaker's Desk Book of Quips, Quotes, and Anecdotes.* Englewood Cliffs, NJ: Prentice-Hall, 1963.

Carnegie, Dale. *The Quick and Easy Way to Effective Speaking.* Garden City, NY: Dale Carnegie and Associates, 1962.

Carnes, William T. *Effective Meetings for Busy People.* New York: McGraw-Hill, 1980.

Davidoff, Henry, editor. *The Pocket Book of Quotations.* New York: Pocket Books, 1952.

Fechtner, Leopold. *5,000 One and Two Liners for Any and Every Occasion.* West Nyack, NY: Parker Publishing, 1973.

Flesch, Rudolf. *How to Write, Speak, and Think More Effectively.* New York: Harper & Row, 1960.

Hilton, Jack and Mary Knoblauch. *On Television! A Survival Guide for Media Interviews.* New York: AMACOM, 1980.

Hodnett, Edward. *Effective Presentations: How to Present Facts, Figures, and Ideas Successfully.* West Nyack, NY: Parker Publishing, 1967.

Howard, Vernon. *Talking to an Audience.* New York: Sterling Publishing, 1963.

Howell, William S. and Ernest G. Borman. *Presentational Speaking for Business and the Professions.* New York: Harper & Row, 1971.

Jay, Anthony. *The New Oratory.* New York: American Management Association, 1971.

Kelley, Joseph J., Jr. *Speechwriting: A Handbook for All Occasions.* New York: New American Library, 1980.

Kemp, Jerrold E. *Planning and Producing Audiovisual Materials.* New York: Thomas Y. Crowell, 1975.

Kenny, Michael. *Presenting Yourself.* New York: John Wiley & Sons, 1982.

Kenny, Peter. *A Handbook of Public Speaking for Scientists & Engineers.* Bristol, England: Adam Hilger Ltd., 1982.

Larson, Orvin. *When It's Your Turn to Speak.* New York: Harper & Row, 1971.

Lieberman, Gerald F. *3,500 Good Jokes for Speakers.* New York: Dolphin Books, 1975.

Linkletter, Art. *Public Speaking for Private People.* Indianapolis: Bobbs-Merrill, 1980.

Lobingier, John L., Jr. *Business Meetings That Make Business.* London: Collier-Macmillan, 1969.

McFarland, Kenneth. *Eloquence in Public Speaking—How to Set Your Words on Fire.* Englewood Cliffs, NJ: Prentice-Hall, 1961.

Mambert, W.A. *Presenting Technical Ideas.* New York: John Wiley & Sons, 1968.

Molloy, John T. *Dress for Success.* New York: Peter H. Wyden, 1975.

———. *The Woman's Dress for Success Book.* New York: Follett, 1977.

Morrisey, George L. *Effective Business and Technical Presentations.* Reading, MA: Addison-Wesley, 1975.

Olmstead, Joseph A. *Small-Group Instruction: Theory and Practice.* Alexandria, VA: Human Resources Organization, 1974.

Oskamp, Stuart. *Attitudes and Opinions.* Englewood Cliffs, NJ: Prentice-Hall, 1977.

Powell, J. Lewis. *Executive Speaking, An Acquired Skill*, revised edition. Washington, D.C.: The Bureau of National Affairs, Inc. 1980.

Rodgers, Natalie H. *Talk Power.* New York: Dodd, Mead & Co., 1982.

Roylance, William H. *I Shoulda Said . . . A Treasury of Insults, Put-Downs, Boasts, Praises, Witticisms, Wisecracks, Comebacks, and Ad-Libs.* West Nyack, NY: Parker Publishing, 1973.

Samovar, Larry A. and Jack Mills. *Oral Communication—Message and Response.* Dubuque, IA: William C. Brown, 1980.

Seldes, George, compiler. *The Great Quotations.* New York: Pocket Books, 1967.

Simmons, S.H. *How To Be the Life of the Podium.* New York: AMACOM, 1982.

Spinrad, Leonard and Thelma. *Speaker's Lifetime Library.* West Nyack, NY: Parker Publishing, 1979.

Sutherland, James, editor. *The Oxford Book of Literary Anecdotes.* New York: Pocket Books, 1975.

Swrydenko, Nicholas and Harvey Wasserman, editors. *The Book of Facts.* New York: Dell Publishing, 1979.

Tacey, William S. *Business and Professional Speaking.* Dubuque, IA: William C. Brown, 1975.

Tarver, Dr. Jerry. *Professional Speech Writing.* Richmond, VA: The Effective Speech Writing Institute, 1982.

Thrash, Artie Adams, Annette N. Shelby, and Jerry L. Tarver. *Speaking Up Successfully.* New York: CBS College Publishing, 1984.

Walter, Otis M. and Robert L. Scott. *Thinking and Speaking*. New York: Macmillan, 1979.

Weiss, Harold and J.B. McGrath, Jr. *Technically Speaking*. New York: McGraw-Hill, 1963.

Williams, William G. *Money-Making Meetings*. Annapolis, MD: Share Publishing, 1982.

Index